88

IDENTIFICATION REQUIRED.

COPY 14

Other TAB books by the author:

No. 2255 *Passing Your Instrument Pilot's Written Exam*
No. 2273 *Cold Weather Flying*
No. 2293 *Instrument Flying*
No. 2318 *How to Become a Flight Engineer*
No. 2345 *Foundations of Flying*

FIRST EDITION

FIRST PRINTING

Copyright © 1984 by TAB BOOKS Inc.

Printed in the United States of America

Reproduction or publication of the content in any manner, without express
permission of the publisher, is prohibited. No liability is assumed with respect to
the use of the information herein.

Library of Congress Cataloging in Publication Data

Griffin, Jeff.
    Pilot's guide to weather forecasting.

    Includes index.
    1. Meteorology in aeronautics.   I. Title.
TL556.G76   1984   629.132'4   83-10589
ISBN 0-8306-2331-0 (pbk.)

Contents

Introduction

The old cliché, "only fools and newcomers try to predict the weather around here," may fit many pilots. In truth, however, most pilots look up to the pilot who can display a working knowledge of weather. In a way, he becomes a pilot's pilot. The reason we learn to "read" the weather, though, is not to impress pilot friends but to enable ourselves to utilize an aircraft fully. Therefore, the main thrust of this book is directed toward making you independent of the forecast you receive before a flight—to be able to say, "The forecast is wrong and this is what I am going to do."

The question comes up again and again: With all of today's technology, why aren't the forecasts always right? If 5,000 skilled and degreed meteorologists cannot produce a 100 percent accurate forecast 100 percent of the time, how can one individual do any better? Well, an individual may not do better all the time, but if he hits when the National Weather Service of the National Oceanic and Atmospheric Administration misses, the overall situation is improved.

We have decided that with all the technology available today, the forecast information should be better. The further a forecast looks into the future, the higher the chances that it will be wrong. We have been living with this sort of thing for years as pilots. Maybe it is time to take a look at the forecasting process and understand the limitations on meteorologists. With this information, we should be able to spot segments as pilots where perhaps we could assist in some way. Also, we will be able to spot the weaknesses and find the areas in which our weather predictions would work to up our flight completion rate.

Until the advent of the computer in the 1950s, forecasting consisted of taking current weather observations. The belief then—and even now to some degree—was that the current weather pattern will lead to the next particular pattern because the past records show this to be the case. Climatology was of utmost importance and essential for making the next day's forecast.

During the 1950s, computers began to take on some of the workload. The trouble back then was that they were incredibly slow compared with those of today. It would take a machine of 1950s vintage 24 hours to produce a 24 hour forecast. With improvements, the computers came to be of more use to the Weather Service. They have augmented man's ability to produce a better product, but not replaced man. Man was and still is very vital to the process.

At 1200 and 0000 Zulu every day of the year, 65 balloons are released within the 48 contiguous states. These balloons ascend at a known rate, so by timing them it is possible to know at what altitude various pressure readings are taken. At the balloon's launch site is a minicomputer capable of recording all the radiosonde's information and tracking it with a direction finder. By tracking the balloon, information on winds aloft is obtained. In addition to pressure and direction, the sonde takes readings of temperature and moisture. From this, calculations of dewpoint, cloud formation, and precipitation are made. At 94,000 feet, the balloon bursts and the radiosonde parachutes to earth. The NWS then hopes that someone will find the sonde, return it to an address that is attached, and guarantees the postage.

All the data from the sonde is, as mentioned, sent to a minicomputer at the launch site. This computer relays the information it receives to Suitland, Maryland, through Kansas City, Missouri. At the same time this is happening, from all over the country, pilot reports and satellite data are fed into the large central computer. It takes about one and one-half hours for the central computer to receive all the upper data from the various balloon sites. After receiving this information, the computer starts to cipher.

Already stored in the computer is a weather history of days and years gone by. Against these records the computer compares today's data. Manipulating all this mathematically, the computer will find a similarity to some weather pattern in the past and produce a vertical and horizontal picture of the atmosphere. In essence, the computer has done the same thing that pre-1950 forecasters did, only with slightly more accuracy.

It takes about one hour for the computer to spit anything out after it starts to cipher. It finally regurgitates a picture of the most important flow altitude, 18,000 feet. Since the whole process began, about two and one-half hours have gone by. Finally, the forecasters have something in their hands to look at. While the forecasters are making their pencil marks on the 18,000-foot picture, the computer goes back to work for another hour. This time it produces forecasts for the next 12, 24, 36, and 48 hours. The information contained is on upper-air flows, thunderstorm activity, precipitation, temperature, dewpoint, visibility, cloud heights and amounts, and pressures aloft and at the surface. During this process the computer places a grid over the entire lower 48 states. This grid divides the country into 90-square-mile segments and the computer makes a forecast for each separate segment.

During all this ciphering, newer information is coming. The forecasters have a chance to look at pilot reports (Pireps) and new satellite pictures. The forecasters then compare the computer printout with the new information. From this they can determine if fronts are moving faster or slower than predicted by the computer. It is always possible that the computer has made an error due to areas of missing input. Many reporting sites can be hundreds of miles apart. A pilot report of an area of colder temperatures or higher winds may be brought to the surface. Thereby the forecaster alters the forecast to fit the new facts. One can see how important Pireps can be in preparing a forecast.

When the computer finally issues its complex weather forecast, it has been four hours since the balloons went up. The forecasters step in and bring it up to date as much as possible with new information. Finally, the whole thing is broadcast to nationwide offices of the Weather Service and to 12 Area Forecast Offices. The upper air information from which the area forecasts are drawn is about 12 hours old when the area forecast offices get it. As a result, the area forecast is not prepared on that information alone. The forecaster uses hourly sequence reports, Pireps, and satellite to observe new trends.

One of the obvious limitations of the computer is that it cannot be programmed with local knowledge of the weather. For example, Traverse City, Michigan, is affected locally during the winter by heavy snows due to lake effect. (Lake effect is cold air blowing across the water and picking up enough moisture to dump generous amounts of snow.) The computer cannot be told that this happens every winter. Instead, it has to learn this statistically. Then and only then will it forecast that condition. Of course, most regional offices recognize this quirk and will change forecasts "manually" to reflect the possibility of lake effect or any other local condition.

Another deficiency in the system is the lack of reporting points in the western U.S. Since there is a larger number of reporting stations in the eastern and central part of the country, those forecasts are more accurate. The meteorologists claim that they can forecast no better than they are able to observe. This is an important point to remember as a pilot forecaster. The western coast of the nation is at a disadvantage. Since the advent of satellites, weather ships have been phased out. Now there are no more observations coming from west of the coast. Hence, weather that is only a couple of hours away from arriving at the coast can be missed or not forecast.

The terminal forecasts are generally more accurate than the area forecasts by virtue of being touched more by the human hand. There are 52 offices that prepare terminal forecasts for 500 airports. These forecasts are prepared in the same way as the area forecast. But local human knowledge plays a more important part. The forecasters tend to know the anachronisms of an area and can adjust a forecast to reflect those eccentricities. Also, terminal forecasts are amended more often.

A seemingly strange thing to us pilots is how a forecast will predict 600 feet and one mile visibility. This keeps us from using the airport as an alternate. Couldn't the forecaster have made it for 600 and two just as easily? Unfortunately, the meterologists don't know what aviation minimums are. They profess that they don't *want* to know them, as that would impose artificial restrictions on them doing their job—and I guess they have a point.

Area forecasts are rarely amended. Only when a significant change is occurring will the meteorologists tear the old one up and throw it away. "Significant weather change" in this case means the skies go from being predicted clear to overcast. The National Weather Service uses Airmets and Sigmets for their revisions of the area forecast instead. (This is why you should always request them at the end of a weather briefing.)

There is a chance that, in the future, the FSS briefer will be taken completely out of the picture. Now under study is a program by which the pilot can talk directly with a computer and get a briefing. This is an effort to eliminate the optimism or pessimism so often injected by the middleman. The program proposes to break the current 90-square-mile grid down to 22 square miles. When the pilot tells the computer his route of flight, the computer will pull up the forecasts for all the squares along that route. I don't know all the details, but I sure would hate to listen to 472 little forecasts just to fly across a state.

The original question was "Why should a pilot try to forecast weather?" The answer is simple. First, who can best see conditions developing, the pilot (who is where they are) or the forecast office hundreds of miles away? The pilot, of course. Second, with up to 12 hours delay in some parts of the forecaster's information, it is bound to lose some accuracy. Third, no one knows the local signs of a weather change better than a local pilot, who can notice the slightest change and prepare his flight plans accordingly. Of course, we don't always fly in the local area, but we do tend to fly the same routes or portions of routes over and over.

The pilot has it hands down over the forecaster when it comes to knowing present conditions. Not detailed in this book is the fact that pilot intuition can be a remarkable guideline to a safe flight. It may not be scientific weather forecasting, but if it is enough to get one to call Flight Watch for an update, it can be worth a lot. But why rely on intuition? In this book are the facts to open up a whole new world of flying and an understanding of the nature of the atmosphere that surrounds us.

Chapter 1

Basic Weather Ingredients

The phone was beginning to ring. I kept thinking how much I hated to give the bad news to my business associate. An important meeting was scheduled over lunch and the last possible minute had just expired that would allow me to fly to a city 300 miles away and arrive on time.

The secretary answered in a most chipper voice, announced the company's name, and asked if there was anything she could do to help.

"Mr. Harold Weston, please," I asked in my most business-like voice. "This is Jeff Griffin, calling long distance."

At last Mr. Weston came on the phone, and I agonizingly told him in simple words that I was socked in due to weather and would not make our scheduled appointment.

"Socked in!" He was exasperated. "For crying out loud, Griffin, it's clear as a bell here. Are you trying to buy time?"

"Well, no, Mr. Weston. But certainly you must realize that it's always clear somewhere." I tried to explain that it was a warm frontal situation, and that its effects had not yet reached his area, but that it would in a matter of time. I wouldn't say I convinced him, but we postponed the date another couple of days. This gave me time to watch the weather and decide early enough to drive if it was necessary.

It's tough being a pilot and trying to get full use out of an airplane when you're only VFR rated. It can be just as frustrating when you're instrumented rated, although not as often. Things such

1

as icing and lines of thunderstorms slow everybody down regardless of their ratings. The poor VFR pilot, though, is affected by just plain cloudy or foggy days.

What we hope to look at in the coming pages are simple methods for forecasting the weather for the immediate future, even up to a day or so in advance. This can translate into forecasting the weather a hundred or so miles up the line when you are already airborne and faced with inflight decisions. Year after year, the statistics show that a major cause of accidents is continuing into adverse weather conditions.

Why do pilots make these same mistakes again and again? The reason is that flight instructors don't put enough emphasis on the importance of being weather-wise. In fact, many newly rated instructor pilots do not have much weather experience to pass on. The fact that you are even reading this book puts you into an elite group of individuals who care and are ambitious enough to find out some things for themselves. Frankly, there is precious little being done to improve the statistics in the area of weather-related accidents. The best hedge against becoming a statistic yourself is to read and learn as much as possible about weather.

Oddly, it is not just the private sector of aviation that is "weather dumb." As a Captain on an airline I have had the experience of seeing just who is experienced. It is truly amazing that many military pilots have little weather experience, when they are most highly sought-after in the civilian market. Perhaps the reason for this is that many are fighter pilots and just don't have to deal with weather as does a transport pilot.

Civilian pilots who come up the rungs of the ladder are often just as poorly prepared. I have noticed that many are limited in experience due to the area in which they have done most of their flying. For example, many West Coast pilots are naive about thunderstorm flying. That's easy enough to understand, because there are few thunderstorms in that part of the country. Southern pilots have inadequate experience in icing conditions. Of course, not all pilots are this way, but it is a tendency that I have noticed.

The most dangerous attitude that you can harbor is one of blind optimism. It is true that on a clear day you can say that the weather will deteriorate eventually, and it is true that on a cloudy, rainy day that the weather will eventually improve, but it may not be reasonable to believe that the clouds will open up and show the ground waiting with open arms or that the blue sky will last through the next hour. This is not meant to sound overly melodramatic, it's just a realistic belief that weather can seem unpredictable if you don't know what to watch for.

Experience in forecasting what the weather will do on the short term can be foremost described as an exercise in the powers of observation. As we all know, weather is a combination of many factors. However, the power to forecast from the present up to about 24 hours distant can be done mainly by using three factors: the wind, the barometric pressure, and cloud types that are present. Understand that things such as lapse rates, position of jet streams, air stability, and relative humidity play great roles in the National Weather Service's ability to predict the weather and make long-term forecasts. If you think about it, though, the three things that you always have instant access to in the cockpit are the wind, barometric pressure, and a wide view of the clouds ahead. Because of this truth, we will pay particular attention to these main factors. However, it is my hope to also impart an understanding of the other main factors.

What Causes the Wind?

Probably one of the reasons that most pilots hate to learn weather is due to the elementary ground one has to cover. After all, all we want to know is whether it is going to go IFR on us or not. The chances of predicting whether it will or not are slim unless you have a good basic foundation on which to build.

Where does the wind come from? It is a basic function of

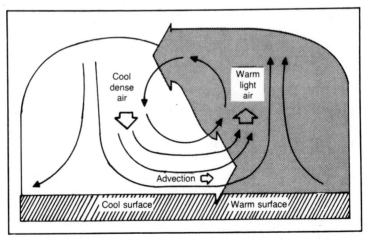

Fig. 1-1. A convective current results from uneven heating of air by contrasting surface temperatures.

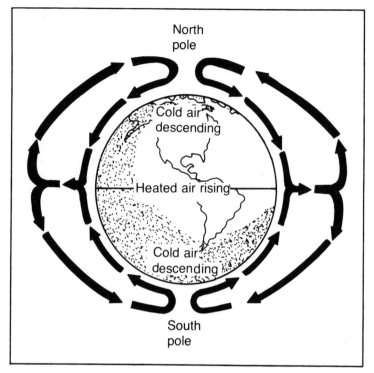

Fig. 1-2. Circulation as it would appear on a non-rotating globe. The less dense air rises from the equator while the more dense air moves from the poles towards the equator.

temperature. Differences in temperature create differences in atmospheric pressure. These pressure differences drive a most complex system of winds in an infinite cycle to reach equilibrium. That sounds very simple, but a great many factors go into the complete picture.

One of those important factors is *convection*. Convection is the unequal heating of the Earth's surface. The heated air becomes less dense, expands, and rises. Denser or cooler air sinks to the ground and replaces the warm air. This cycle of convective circulation will continue as long as uneven heating occurs (Fig. 1-1).

Sure, you say that's how thermals are made. Sailplane pilots take advantage of this activity daily. Well, that is true; however, this convective circulation can and does occur on a large scale. Look at Fig. 1-2. It shows how heated air starts at the equator and cools over the poles. If the planet Earth did not rotate, as it does, we would have north winds in the northern hemisphere all the time.

However, a thing called the *Coriolis force* changes the look of the atmosphere from simple to complex.

One of the laws of motion, as described by Newton, is that a moving mass will travel in a straight line unless it is acted upon by some outside force. However, if one views the moving mass from a rotating platform, the path of the mass relative to the platform appears to be deflected or curved. To illustrate this point, imagine a phonograph turntable turning very slowly. Let's pretend we draw a line with chalk straight out from the center with a ruler. As we draw the line with the chalk, it obviously travels straight. However, when we stop the record we can see a line that spirals outward from the center of the turntable or record (Fig. 1-3). If we were viewing this process from the center of the turntable, it would appear that some force had deflected the chalk to the right.

A similar apparent force deflects moving particles on the Earth, namely the atmosphere. Because of the Earth's near-spherical shape, the effects become much more complex than our

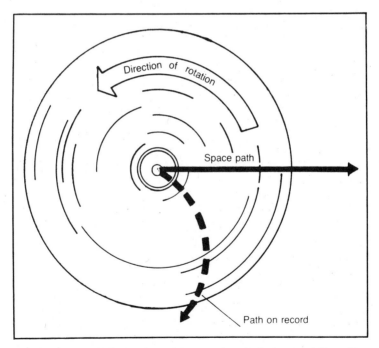

Fig. 1-3. Apparent deflective force due to rotation of a horizontal platform. The space path is the path taken by a piece of chalk. The dashed line on the record is the traced pattern of the chalk. Relative to the record, the chalk appeared to curve; it actually traveled a straight line.

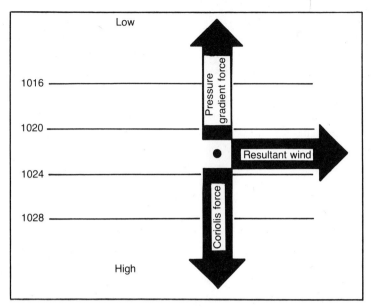

Fig. 1-4. The effect of Coriolis force on wind relative to the isobars. The pressure gradient is balanced when Coriolis force deflects the wind.

turntable example. Every time we fly we must deal with this force, for it affects the paths of aircraft, missiles, birds, ocean currents and—most important to us—the air currents. The Coriolis force deflects air to the right in the Northern Hemisphere and to the left in the Southern Hemisphere.

Coriolis force operates at right angles to the wind's direction and is directly proportional to wind speed. Increase the wind speed and the Coriolis force increases. At a given latitude, double the wind speed and you double the Coriolis force.

As we just mentioned the Coriolis force becomes maximum at some latitude. This is because it varies from zero at the equator to a maximum at the poles. In other words, the Coriolis force has no effect on winds at the equator, but has a pronounced effect at the middle and high latitudes.

Earlier we discussed the pressure gradient that drives the wind and we said it was perpendicular to the isobars. When a pressure gradient force is first established, wind begins to blow from the high pressure center to the low pressure center directly across the isobars. But the instant the wind begins to move, it is veered to the right by the Coriolis force and exactly balances the pressure gradient force as shown in Fig. 1-4.

The General Circulation

Understanding the general circulation pattern of the northern hemisphere is important because it explains why the weather changes in North America as it does. To begin with, air is forced aloft at the equator. Because the sun's rays reach the polar areas at a greater angle than at the equator, the air cannot be warmed as easily. The result is that the air cools and thus sinks. What begins to take form is a large convective current covering half the globe. The overall pattern would be of two convective currents, one in each of the northern and southern hemispheres.

But this simple model is not the reality. The two currents we have will be disturbed by the Coriolis force. Let us concentrate on the northern hemisphere. As the heated air begins its trek to the north it is turned to the right. At about 30 degrees of latitude the wind becomes westerly. This blocks further northward movement. At the same time there is air over the poles starting to move southward. This air is also deflected to the right and becomes an east wind. This halts its southerly progress. The result is piles of air at about 30 degrees and 60 degrees of latitide. The weight of these "piles of air" can be translated into higher pressure or a high pressure belt. Figures 1-5 and 1-6 show the subtropical high pressure belts during January and July near 30 degrees latitude in both hemispheres.

The trouble with these semipermanent high pressure belts is that they disrupt the natural convection transfer between equator and poles. A simple law of physics states that disturbed fluids will strive to reach equilibrium. The atmosphere is a fluid and thus strives to reach equilibrium. The subtropical high pressure belt tends to block this search for equilibrium and something must give. The effect is that huge masses of air begin overturning in middle latitudes to complete the exchange. We know these air masses as *cold fronts* (air that is moving southward and colder relative to the air it is overtaking) as they move southward. Large mid-latitude storms develop between cold fronts and carry warm air northward. The upshot of this quest for equilibrium is a band of migratory storms in the mid-latitudes with ever-changing weather.

Pressure differences cause wind as we discussed early on, and seasonal pressure variations determine to a great extent the areas of these cold air outbreaks and mid-latitude storms. But seasonal pressure variations are largely due to seasonal temperature changes. We discussed earlier how warm surface temperatures greatly relate to low pressure, and cold temperatures, high pres-

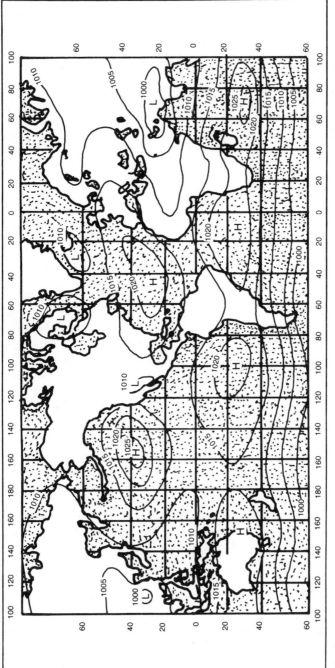

Fig. 1-5. Mean worldwide surface pressure distribution in July. The warm land areas are affected by low pressure; the cooler oceanic areas tend to be affected by high pressure.

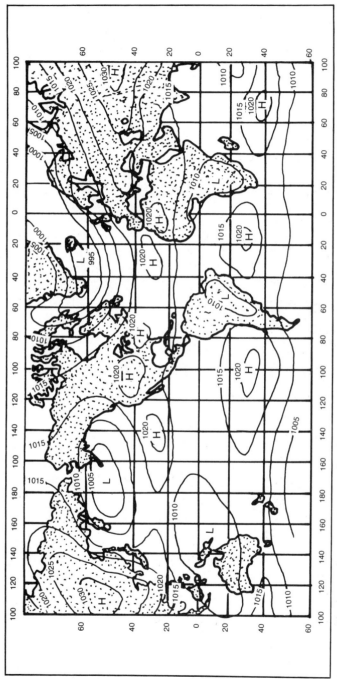

Fig. 1-6. Mean worldwide surface pressure distribution in January. The cooler land regions are of predominantly high pressure while the warmer oceanic regions are dominated by low pressure.

9

sure. We must understand that seasonal temperatures over the continents are much greater than over oceans.

Summer usually means the land areas will be the areas of low pressure and the relatively cooler oceans will propagate the high pressure areas. When winter comes around, however, the reverse is true. The high pressure moves over the continents and the low pressure moves out over the oceans.

In the summer, referring to what we have just stated above, the weather disturbances that move along the mid-latitudes are weak and more likely to originate from cool water surfaces. You may have noticed that in late spring or early fall that the television weatherman refers often to the cold fronts as *Pacific fronts*. This is the reason.

When winter sets in, though, the weather disturbances or fronts tend to originate in the colder continental regions. These cold outbreaks tend to be the strongest when compared to their warm weather counterparts. Often the TV weatherman will refer to these as *Canadian* and *Polar air masses* which indicate the continental region of their origin.

Direction of Flow around Pressure Systems

Have you ever wondered why the wind circles the high and low pressure systems in the directions it does? Well, our winds generally flow from areas of high pressure to areas of low pressure. Thus, as the air flows outward directly from the center of a high pressure area, it is deflected to the right by the Coriolis force. The result is a clockwise flow and the system is called an *anticyclone*.

The storms that develop between high pressure systems are, of course, low pressure systems. The wind in these systems blows inward toward the center. Once again the Coriolis force works its magic and deflects the wind to the right. The resultant flow is in a counterclockwise direction or *cyclonic* flow. The system is called a *cylcone*.

Probably the most important point made so far is that the winds flow from a high to a low. They also tend to parallel the isobars on the charts. This is not their natural inclination, but is caused by the Coriolis force.

Friction

Usually, friction is a force that is overlooked when discussing wind. The friction between the wind and the terrain slows the wind. The rougher the terrain, the greater the frictional effect. Also, according to physics, the stronger the wind, the greater the friction. Friction always works opposite to the surface wind's direction.

An interesting thing happens as friction slows the wind. The Coriolis force on the wind is also decreased, but the pressure gradient force is not affected. The net effect is that the pressure gradient and Coriolis forces are no longer in balance. The stronger pressure gradient force turns the wind at an angle across the isobars toward lower pressure. Essentially, the wind veers back to the left. The angle of surface wind is about 10 degrees over water, increasing according to the roughness of the terrain. This is the reason that winds aloft forecasts usually reflect a wind more from the right (increasingly from the west) at each higher forecast level.

The Jet Stream

No discussion of wind would be complete without mention of the *jet stream*. On the average, winds increase with altitude until we reach the *tropopause*. The tropopause is the boundary between the *troposphere* in which most of us fly and the *stratosphere* generally penetrated by jets. The winds reach a maximum near the tropopause. Further, these winds tend to band into narrow areas or cores and meander north and south near the level of the tropopause (Figs. 1-7, 1-8). Ordinarily, you won't be bothered by these winds as a general aviation pilot. However, it is a mistake to overlook them because the jet streams (and often there are more than one) are the *steering* winds for all major storm systems. To have aware-

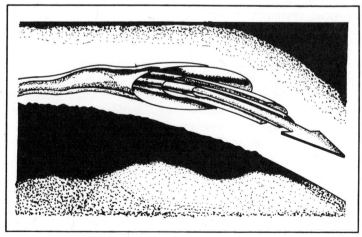

Fig. 1-7. Artist's conception of the jet stream. The arrow shows the direction of wind flow.

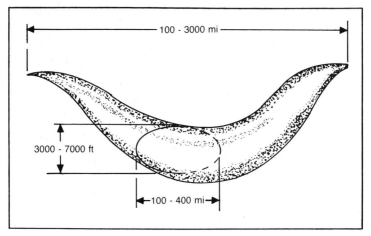

Fig. 1-8. A segment of the jet stream.

ness of the position of the jet is to greatly increase your ability to forecast the weather.

Local and Small-Scale Winds

Although local or small-scale winds don't affect the weather very often in a major way, they can be of importance to you in controlling the type of ride and landings you're going to get. Flying in the mountains can be an extremely challenging, enlightening, and beautiful experience. However, some understanding of the type of winds that haunt the wilderness can contribute to a passenger's enjoyment of the ride. Fundamentally, there are two types of winds in the mountains. They are known as *mountain* and *valley winds*. They work like this:

In the daytime, air next to the mountain slopes is heated by radiation from the sun. The air at the same altitude but out in the valley away from the rocks remains comparatively cooler. The effect is that the cooler, more dense air settles toward the valley floor. The warmer air is thereby forced upslope and the wind staying essentially next to the rocks is moved out of the valley. This condition is known as the valley wind.

The opposite condition occurs at night when the owls are out searching for prey. As the sun disappears behind the last peak, radiation cooling begins to take place. The cool air sinks along the slopes, resulting in a mountain wind that rustles the spruce and fir trees outside the window. If you're out flying, it is best to remember where the wind may be most likely to come from. In the daytime the

12

Fig. 1-9. The Chinook is a katabatic wind. This means it moves downslope. As the air moves downslope, it is warmed. This sometimes causes dramatic warming of the plains east of the Rockies.

wind will tend to come from the center of the valleys and at night from the direction of the nearest mountain.

Katabatic Wind

One mountain wind that is not so pleasant is the *katabatic wind*. Ordinarily, these have interesting or exotic names like the *Bora* that blows from the Alps to the Mediterranean coast. Closer to home we have the *Chinook* that blows from the eastern slopes of the Rockies out onto the Great Plains, and the *Santa Ana* which comes down the slopes of the Sierra Nevadas into the Santa Ana Valley (Figs. 1-9, 1-10).

What is a katabatic wind? It's a wind that blows down an incline.

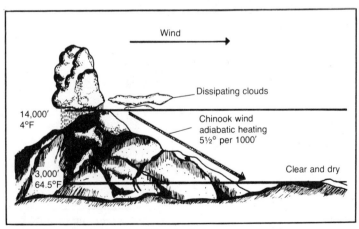

Fig. 1-10. Another look at the Chinook wind.

Therefore, the mountain wind is a katabatic wind. Any katabatic wind is due to cold air cascading down the mountain slopes and displacing warmer, less dense air ahead of it. Air is heated and dried as it flows downslope, hence the dramatic warming that the Chinook and Santa Ana bring.

Some Simple Yet Often Overlooked Facts

As we have discussed, winds are related most often to pressure systems. Also, low pressure systems are generally associated with poor weather. Let's examine why this occurs. At the surface, the wind flows from high pressure to low pressure (Fig. 1-11). Whenever the air converges at the low pressure center, it cannot go outward against the pressure gradient, nor can it go downward into the ground. The only direction it can go is *upward!* Therefore, a low or trough is an area of rising air.

I have had argument after argument at my airline on this point. It seems there is a question on our annual recurrent training exam about the direction of flow out of a low. I always "miss" the answer to this question because the training department is in error. I always ask these two questions to prove my point: Is a tornado a low or high pressure phenomena? *It is a low pressure system*, they answer. Which direction does debris go inside a tornado? *It goes up*, they

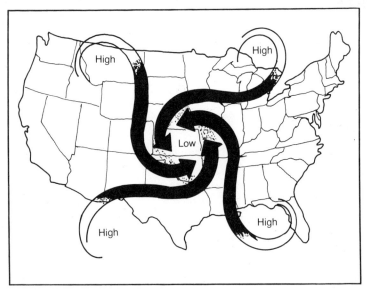

Fig. 1-11. Wind tends to flow from a high to a low. As shown, the wind will cross the isobars at an angle.

say. Then which way does the air go in a low pressure system? *Oh, gee, I guess that's right.* Do they change the question next year? Are you kidding?

Well, anyway, the point is that air rises in a low pressure area. As we all know, rising air will often cause clouds and precipitation if there is enough moisture available. Thus, the correlation between low pressure and bad weather.

Using similar reasoning, we can determine that high pressure areas are areas of descending air and hence not conducive to cloud formation on a broad plane. The correlation here is good weather.

A very important point is that often there are pressure systems, either high or low, that dominate the upper air. More often than not the upper air systems bear more responsibility for our weather than do the surface systems. Those systems that "deepen" and reach from surface up into the upper level (which is about 18,000 feet or the 500 millibar level) are the most intense.

Although features of the high altitude charts and the surface map are related, they are seldom identical. In fact, an upper air pattern may not show up at all on the surface map and vice versa.

What we are discussing here is extremely important to the pilot in summer. Widespread cloudiness and precipitation will build in front of an upper trough or low. A line of showers and thunderstorms is very common with such an upper pattern. The amazing thing is that there may not be even a single ripple on the surface map. This situation is extremely common throughout the Great Plains during the Spring. It has been the cause of much destruction. The wary pilot checks the upper air charts.

Consider the upper high pressure patterns. They can be equally devastating in summer. The record heat wave of 1980 is a case in point. An upper air high pressure tends to place a "cap" on the convection process. Upward motion is inhibited by the sinking air of high pressure systems that we discussed a few paragraphs back. We then begin to have a stagnant pattern, sometimes with fog, low stratus, and haze. If there is a moderate surface wind, which is the pattern we had in the summer of 1980, good flying weather prevails, though I must admit that density altitude becomes a factor. And unfortunately, little precip falls on crops and reservoirs and the result is a hot and dry summer.

Highs and lows tend to lean from the surface into the upper atmosphere. Because of this slope, winds aloft blow across the associated surface systems. The upper winds tend to steer surface systems in the general direction of the upper wind flow. A lone thunderstorm moves in the direction that the wind "blows off" its top or the "anvil head."

Intense, cold, low pressure systems tend to lean less than the weaker systems. If the storm is intense enough it will be aligned almost vertically through the atmosphere. The resultant maps will show low pressure at the surface and at altitude in the same area. The upper winds tend to encircle the surface low and hence do not blow across it as in the example above. The upshot is that the storm system moves slowly, causing extensive and persistent areas of cloudiness, precipitation, and strong winds. The term *cold low* is sometimes used by the weatherman to describe this sort of system.

In contrast to the cold low, we find the term *thermal low*. This kind of system forms over a dry, sunny region warming from surface heating, and thus causing a low pressure area. The warm air is carried to high levels of convection, but clouds are scarce due to lack of moisture. Since in warmer air pressure decreases with altitude, the warm surface low does not manifest itself at the upper levels. Unlike the cold low, the thermal low is weak and relatively shallow. No well-defined cyclonic circulation usually develops. We generally have good flying weather in areas of thermal lows, but it is bumpy. So basically there are three exceptions to the low pressure/bad weather, high pressure/good weather precept: (1) we can experience cloudiness and precipitation with an upper air trough or low that does not make itself apparent on the surface map. (2) We have the contaminated or stagnant high pressure system. (3) The thermal low. All of these may not produce IFR condition, but they all can and do produce uncomfortable flying conditions of some kind.

If there is a lesson from all this, it should be to consult the 500 millibar chart. The areas of low pressure presented on this chart are generally more indicative of the conditions to follow than the surface maps.

Something of Great Use

Now that we've talked about wind and pressure systems, we need to illustrate some use for them in forecasting. After all, that's what this book is about. Among the handiest forecast tools at the simple observation level are the *crossed-winds rules*. These rules are of most value on the ground while you do your preflight, yet you can with light mental gymnastics use them to your advantage in the cockpit. (I would suspect, though, that most of us would not use them in the air.) The advantages of the crossed-winds rules is that you may apply them when you are in the outback where weather

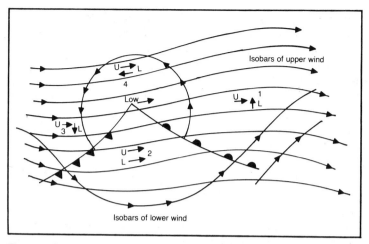

Fig. 1-12. An overlay of the upper winds to the lower winds. A low pressure center at the surface is shown with its associated fronts. See text for further explanation.

information is scarce, or use them a day or two in advance of a flight without bothering the FSS.

Variable, and frequently IFR conditions, will result as the product of a succession of low pressure systems crossing over an area. Surface winds will tend to "back" or move counterclockwise when the weather is deteriorating and "veer" or move clockwise whenever the weather is to improve. We have discussed this earlier. The problem is, though, that this is a rather vague way of telling the weather's future. Looking at Fig. 1-12 you'll see what I mean. On the extreme right of the illustration, notice that the wind is moving counterclockwise or backing as fair weather comes along. Also notice that the winds veer south of the low and back north of the low as the low passes.

You can make much better use of Fig. 1-12 if you use the crossed-winds rules. The illustration depicts an eastward moving depression moving under the impetus of upper winds. There are two associated fronts—a cold front and warm front with a warm sector in between the two. The wind moves parallel to the isobars and is labeled (L) for lower and (U) for upper level winds.

At point 1 we see the upper and lower winds are crossed at right angles. The depression is not far behind to the west and the associated warm front will arrive later. At location 3, the winds are also crossed but in the opposite direction. Location 3 is behind the cold front where really cold air is flowing in. This area will eventually change from blustery and showery conditions to fair weather.

Basically then, location 1 will deteriorate and 3 will improve. But how can we figure that out if we don't know which side of a low we are on?

Well, enter the crossed-winds rules:

☐ Stand with your back to the lower wind. Watch the movement of the highest clouds you can see (generally cirrus). If they are coming from the left hand, the weather will normally deteriorate.

☐ Stand with your back to the lower wind. Once again observe the movement of the upper clouds. If they move from the right hand, the weather is improving or due to improve.

Standing with your back to the lower wind is not always as easy as it seems. We have already discussed Coriolis force and friction effects on wind. These will cause the wind to come from slightly different angles, not to mention land or sea breezes or mountain and valley winds. Thus the best way to find the correct lower wind is to pick low level stratus or fair weather cumulus and use their direction of travel for the low level wind.

At positions 2 and 4 there is a definite problem. The winds, upper and lower, are parallel or in opposite directions. This can only mean that no frontal passage is due in the near future.

☐ Stand with your back to the lower wind. If the upper winds move on a parallel course, the weather will not change very much.

Hints on recognizing the direction and speed of the upper winds from cloud formations will be given in the next chapter on clouds.

Chapter 2

Clouds and All They Stand For

Wishing on a cloud, "Cloud Nine," "Chief Thundercloud," cloudy eyes. Clouds have captured the imagination of man for ages. But only a hundred or so years ago man first began to scientifically analyze cloud patterns as harbingers of weather.

All clouds form for some reason, some physical law of nature. When you realize that the type of cloud is an indication of future or present weather, you have cut off a big hunk of the unknown about weather forecasting—at least in the short term.

Ordinarily, clouds will give us some educated guesses as to what the weather will be to about 36 hours hence. Of course, we can't walk outside and say, "that's a cumulus; it's going to snow tomorrow." We must observe clouds hour after hour in order to detect changes that may not fit our first determination. In the case of being airborne, it's not so much observing hour after hour, but mile after mile. Transiting towards the rear of a cold front for example, will show changes rapidly as the front is approached.

All right, you say, but I can't tell one cloud from another. It's easy if you just read on and sort the information into separate pockets. First, clouds occur in all reaches of the atmosphere. Thus they have been separated into three types: low, middle, and high. That should be simple enough, but add specific names to the clouds and some of us get them confused. All high clouds have the prefix *cirro*. Middle clouds have the prefix *alto* and easily remembered low clouds have no prefix.

Additionally, all clouds are further divided into two major

types: *stratus* or layered, and *cumulus* or puffy. Then we put the prefix and the type together, to name our clouds. For instance, a high, thin layered cloud would be called *cirrostratus*. Take a look at the chart below. I think you will see what I mean.

Height Division	Usual Altitude (feet in thousands)	Name
High (Cirro)	20-40	Cirrus
	20-40	Cirrostratus
	20-40	Cirrocumulus
Medium (Alto)	6-20	Altostratus
	6-20	Altocumulus
	6-20	Nimbostratus
Low	0-2	Stratus
	1-5	Cumulus
	1-4.5	Stratocumulus
	1-5	Cumulonimbus

Now, there may be a couple of things about the chart you might have noticed that we didn't talk about before we got to it—one, the word *nimbo* or *nimbus*. Well, I'm afraid this is just another term to remember, but it is easy. Nimbo is applied to a cloud name whenever there is rain falling from that cloud. Secondly, we combined the two terms strato and cumulus together to make stratocumulus. These clouds are neither layered nor billowy or puffy. Thus they remain in a class of their own.

Essentially, if you have learned all the above, you will have enough knowledge on hand to adequately name every type of cloud that you see. There are some types, however, that don't fit into the general naming pattern. The only way to remember them is usually by rote. They are easier to learn, though, if you really see one and remember its characteristics. The two main odd types are *floccus* and *castellanus*. Floccus is a form of altocumulus associated with thundery weather. They reasemble a flock of wooly sheep, hence their name.

Castellanus are also altocumulus clouds. However, they are ordinarily found in a single line and are quite vertically developed. These clouds almost always precede thundery outbreaks as much as eight to ten hours in advance. Hence they are good predictors of thunderstorm occurrence. A helpful hint is to look for these clouds early in the morning, around sunrise.

Pannus, another term to at least recognize, is a low stratus type of cloud. This cloud is formed by turbulent wind eddies lifting and cooling the airspace below a cloud base from which rain, snow or sleet is falling. The latter will not necessarily reach the ground, as it evaporates as it falls and so moistens the airspace. Pannus will foretell immediate rain, but once it has begun to rain in earnest it may extend into total cover at 1,000 feet or so.

What Various Cloud Types Can Tell You

When discussing the high clouds, you need to realize a couple of things. First, and most importantly, they generally forecast the approach or passing of major storm systems. Often, this is done by reading the *fallstreaks*, which brings up the second point. Fall-streaks are "showers" of ice crystals falling from cirrus clouds. These crystals fall through many thousands of feet of the upper air. As they sink, they become deflected by lower level winds which are generally stronger than those above when they are ahead of bad weather systems. Thus these fallstreaks trail from the heads of clouds that precipitated them. Due to the interrelation of winds and temperatures of air masses, the tails of the streaks tend to point toward the warmer air mass. Thus the fallstreaks ahead of a warm front often point southwest. Whenever you see cirrus and associated fallstreaks behind a cold front, they will ordinarily point southeast. These rules are handy in identifying the position of storms, especially when coupled with the crossed-winds rules.

Cirrus

These thin wispy clouds are blown into streaks as we just discussed, and are often known as "mares tails." Cirrus clouds are generally formed by warm, moist, tropical maritime air being lifted up at the polar front over cold, drier polar air. Even at altitudes of 30,000 feet or more, there is enough moisture left to form tiny ice crystals that are the embodiment of this cloud genus. The major inference is for the weather to deteriorate as a major system approaches from the west or a warm front from the southwest.

There are some major clues offered us by these clouds if you look for them.

☐ Organization: If the fallstreaks are fairly streaming in one direction, you can take this to mean that the coming deterioration will take place rather rapidly (Fig. 2-1).

☐ Using the crossed-wind rule, you can determine with your back to the surface wind and if the upper wind is coming from the left that a warm front is to the west and on the way.

Fig. 2-1. Cirrus fallstreaks point to the warmer air mass.

(*Note:* We will discuss warm fronts in detail later, but please note that the passage of a warm front means a cold front is directly behind it.)

☐ Good visibility and possible cumulus clouds present will show the air mass to be polar in nature and will have a strong contrast in temperatures. A wide gap in temperatures, remember, usually means a great variance in pressure and therefore strong winds.

As we mentioned earlier, there are three things to which you have ready access to help forecast weather conditions in the cockpit. They are wind, pressure, and clouds. (Actually, there are more, all related, such as visibility, precip and temperature.) In Table 2-1 we have listed all these factors and what the expected change could be. All data is based on a general aviation aircraft flying at 120 knots, westbound (181 degrees to 359 degrees) or eastbound (0 degrees to 180 degrees) below 10,000 feet. The crossed-winds rules are mentioned again in the category of wind and its associated trend. For crossed-winds work in the cockpit, get the winds aloft forecast for your chosen altitudes and 18,000 and 30,000 feet as well. With this information you will be able to judge the direction of the upper wind and determine if it is backing or veering.

I feel the best way to put Table 2-1 to use is to note the Flight Time column. If your estimated time to your destination is less than the time estimated for the weather to change, then there is a good possibility that the trip can be completed as intended. Or, on the other hand, an alternate course of action can be considered before time runs out.

You may have noticed the below-10,000-feet section of the chart. Since most general aviation pilots fly down in this part of the atmosphere, we choose 10,000 feet as a cutoff. Also, with all due respect to the inexperienced, most of the pilots flying high-dollar turbine equipment have already gained much weather flying wisdom and don't need this sort of chart. However, this chart can make the road to experience easier and safer. It might even make the experience enjoyable. I wish I had had one when I started out.

Table 2-1 was for westbound aircraft. What about eastbound? Well, cirrus clouds such as those pictured in Fig. 2-1 are usually the vanguard of approaching storm systems. We use the word "approaching" here as if we were stationary on the ground. Since, in the northern hemisphere, storms approach from the west or northwest, only a westbound plane would fly towards the deteriorating weather indicated by the cirrus. Eastbound planes would fly from very good to excellent weather until approaching another system from behind. Since that would possibly mean 300—500 miles, it is useless to discuss the possibilities. You must admit our average stage length in general aviation is less than 500 miles.

As we said, there is a possibility that cirrus can mean that you are approaching the back of a front. Whenever this is the case, you will be eastbound and conditions will change much faster and in the opposite sequence from the westbound chart.

Table 2-1. Cirrus and Cirrostratus.

Component	Trend	Below 10,000′	Flight Time	Danger of	Possibly
Wind	Backing and increasing	4-16 knots SW bcmg 5-28 knots S-SE	1-3 hours	35-45 knots	10-15 knots in summer if depression weak
Visibility	Increase then decrease	10-12 miles or more bcmg 2-4 miles in rain or ½ −1 mile in snow	2-3 hours	Fog	4-6 miles in light rain
Precipitation	Rain or snow	Continuous light to moderate	2-4 hours	Heavy rain TRW summer	Slight rain if depression weak
Cloud	Increasing to overcast	8/8 cirro stratus, then 8/8 altostratus, 8/8 nimbostratus with stratocu and pannus	2-4 hours	8/8 low stratus	Broken clouds if depression is weak
Temperature	Cooler	Noticeable drop crossing front	2-3 hours	Bitter in winter and icing	Little change if depression is weak
Pressure	Falling	Rapid fall near front	2-6 hours	Major fall low ground-speeds	Slow fall if depression weak

Table 2-2. Cirrostratus and Altostratus.

Component	Trend	Below 10,000'	Flight Time	Danger of	Possibly
Wind	Increase and backing	18-25 knots SW to SE	1-3 hours	20-35 knots	4-20 knots
Visibility	Decrease	2-4 miles in rain, ½-1 mile if snow	1-2½ hours	½ mile rain zero in snow	Fog
Precipitation	Rain or snow	Begin light and intermittent, bcmg continuous	1-1½ hours	Heavy near front	Drizzle or freezing rain
Cloud	Increasing	8/8 altostratus and nimbostratus	½ hour	8/8 low stratus in 1.5 hours	Broken layers
Temperature	Cooler then warming behind front	Possible inversions	1-2 hours	Colder before frontal passage	Hot in summer
Pressure	Falling	Slower groundspeeds	2-4 hours	Rapid fall if depression strong	Slow if 4-8 knots wind

In Table 2-2 and Fig. 2-2, we'll explore the possibilities of inclement weather as a warm front or occlusion approaching. The clouds in Fig. 2-2 indicate a deterioration of moderate intensity. Note the jet contrails crisscrossing the sky in the foreground. This indicates fairly abundant moisture is aloft at high altitudes. Just below the plane there is a deck of altostratus which is the lowest cloud pictured. The upper wind is fairly strong and across the highest contrail as it is quickly being widened and diffused. The fact that the clouds seen just below the airplane's wings are fairly solid and overcast (referring to the cirrostratus) indicates a fairly well-organized warm front. Another fact that is particularly pertinent is that the axis of the altostratus deck is aligned with the cirrus axis above. This means the upper wind is at right angles to the middle wind because cirrus streams with wind and altostratus lays across the wind which is normal for stable clouds. The snow on the mountains and foreground of Fig. 2-2 indicate winter is the season. Moderate to heavy snow is possible and fog is an even greater possibility, especially across higher terrain.

In summer, you can expect rain out of such a system. Also, you can expect the precipitation, regardless of season, to start out light and intermittent, becoming more heavy as the front nears or you near the front. Warm fronts can create problems for days in an area as they generally move slower than their cold sisters which are bringing up the rear.

Most important about this type of sky is to expect deteriora-

Fig. 2-2. Signs of a warm front in the offing.

Fig. 2-3. Cirrus and altostratus.

tion. Also, if you are traveling towards the front, expect the changes to be a slow process.

In Fig. 2-3 we see cirrus clouds once again. In this instance, though, the sky is showing signs of improving weather. Cirrus clouds are not always bearers of bad news. The fallstreaks tell us the depression is to the east. Remember, fallstreaks point to the area of warmer air. In this case they are pointing SE.

In the other areas of Fig. 2-3, we see altostratus parallel to the cirrus. From this you can expect a cold front moving out of the area. The fractostratus to the left of the palm trees indicate the main precipitation pattern has broken. From Fig. 2-3 you could infer that early evening showers are a possibility, especially if you are westbound, but good VFR is the indication for the most part.

If you use the crossed-winds rules in this case, you would find the cold front had moved through and that colder air is moving into the area. Westbound, you should expect improving weather overall (Table 2-3). Eastbound travel, on the other hand, may give you a rather abrupt change for the worse (Table 2-4).

Sneaking up on the backside of fronts can give the inexperienced pilot a fit. Warm fronts, as you may already know, have wide and bodacious warning signals when approaching from the front. Cold fronts also have their peculiar signposts when approaching them head-on. However, flying toward a front from the backside can be a situation requiring a much higher recognition factor of the clouds and a quick, decisive mind.

Generally, as you approach any front (warm and cold), you will first begin to see fair weather cumulus. Unfortunately, this is often

Table 2-3. Cirrus and Altostratus (Westbound).

Component	Trend	Below 10,000'	Flight Time	Danger of	Possibly
Wind	Decreasing	8-20 knots less at night	Within 3 hours	Rapid rise in pressure, bcmg windy	Instability showers
Cloud	Decreasing	Fractostratus 1/8 to 2/8 coverage	Within 1 hour	Low stratus	No clouds below 10,000'
Pressure	Rising		3 hours	Rapid rise followed by rapid fall	Very small change if system weak
Visibility	No change		3 hours	Fog in low lying areas	Good
Precipitation	Showers until dark	Light in intensity	1/2 to 2 hours	Moderate	No showers
Temperature	Cooler	Watch for ice	1-3 hours	Freezing drizzle	Little change

Table 2-4. Cirrus and Altostratus (Eastbound).

Component	Trend	Below 10,000'	Flight Time	Danger of	Possibly
Wind	Increasing	8-20 knots increasing to as much as 40 knots	½-1 hour	Vertical windshears in TRWs	Change to right near front
Cloud	Increasing	8/8 coverage of stratus	1 hour	Imbedded cumulonimbus	Only middle or high clouds
Pressure	Falling		½-1 hour	Rapid fall if system is strong	Small drop
Visibility	Decreasing	Very low in precipitation	1 hour	½ mile or less in snow	Greater than 3 miles
Precipitation	Increasing	Rain or snow	1-3 hours	Heavy near front	Only light
Temperature	Warming	May still be cold enough for icing	1-3 hours	Heavy ice	Little change

overlooked as a signal and I am as guilty as anyone. But soon, the sky ahead will take on the appearance of a gray wall and fracto clouds will begin to float by below. Usually, fractured clouds indicate the recent presence of precipitation of some form. If you next run into precip prior to encountering clouds at the 3,000 to 10,000 foot level, you can expect them in the next few miles. In the winter, this might translate into icing problems before reaching your destination. In the summer, imbedded thunderstorms are a possibility and we all know what *that* means—no man's land!

Cirrocumulus

Cirrocumulus clouds give us the pretty mackerel sky. As with all cumulus clouds, they are puffy. Cirrocumulus means a puffy cirrus cloud. Whenever a cloud becomes vertically developed, this means there is some sort of lifting action.

Cirrocumulus clouds can be caused by two things. One is high-level frontal activity associated with unstable moist air. The other may be a general upward transition of moist unstable air over higher layers when a heated land surface forces the lower layers to expand.

Cirrocumulus clouds are often associated with a change in the weather, though more often than not the coming deterioration is not intense or prolonged. The old rhyme, "Mackerel sky, mackerel sky—not long wet and not long dry," completely says it all. Altocumulus may often join the same sky ahead of a depression. The way to differentiate the two is to look for shading on the bottom of

Table 2-5. Cirrocumulus.

Component	Trend	Below 10,000'	Flight Time	Danger of	Possibly
Wind	Increase	10-15 knots increase	1 hour	30 knots	No change
Cloud	Bcmg broken altocumulus	Very few clouds	2 hours	Full coverage imbedded TRWs	Decrease in coverage
Pressure	Little change		1-4 hours	Rapid fall near system core	Rising in better wx
Visibility	Remain good	Slight chance for haze layer	2-4 hours	Decrease to MVFR in precipitation	Unlimited
Precipitation	Intermittent	Slight chance of ice near 10,000'	3-4 hours	Heavy TRWs	None
Temperature	Little change	Daily variation		Cool in rain	Warming

the cloud. Altocumulus clouds will be slightly gray and cirrocumulus will not.

Tables 2-5 can postulate a couple of things when combined with the cross-winds rules. Whenever the winds are parallel and not crossed at all, then no great change can be expected—at least for many flight miles. Whenever the winds are crossed for deterioration, the precipitation will likely be heavy.

The presence of cirrocumulus clouds points to unstable air aloft (Fig. 2-4). Unstable air is that which is readily lifted as opposed to stable air which tends to remain flat and resist lifting. Whenever lifting is probable, then so is turbulence. Under these conditions, thunderstorms are likely when the main body of the depression arrives.

Altocumulus

In logical progression from the highest to the lowest, we are now going to examine the middle clouds. Altocumulus are the great

Fig. 2-4. Cirrocumulus, a sign of warm, moist, unstable air aloft.

Table 2-6. Altocumulus.

Component	Trend	Below 10,000'	Flight Time	Danger of	Possibly
Wind	Increasing	10-30 knots	2-4 hours	50 knots at altitude	Little change
Cloud	Increasing	6/8 altocumulus to 8/8 altostratus	1-4 hours	8/8 low stratus	No lower clouds
Pressure	Falling	Steady fall	Immediately	Rapid fall w/strong depression	Slight fall
Visibility	Decreasing	4 to 5 miles bcmg 2 miles	3 hours	¼ mile in fog and drizzle	Unchanged
Precipitation	Intermittent then steady	Rain or snow possible to climb out of light precipitation	2-4 hours	Imbedded TRWs	No precipitation
Temperature	Warming	Some inversions	1-4 hours	Icing in lower clouds	No noticeable change

forebearers of the warm front. When you see altocumulus in the sky, you can almost count on murky weather in as little as 100 flight miles (Table 2-6).

Altocumulus are easy to spot. Usually, they hang close to each other with spaces of sky around each cloud. They have the appearance of mud that has dried out and contracted, leaving each cloud isolated from the next (Fig. 2-5). They are essentially numerous islands in the sky and above 6,000 or 8,000 feet. Ordinarily, they are closer to the 15,000-foot level.

As we mentioned before, vertical development requires the presence of an unstable air mass. If the air mass is unstable, the

Fig. 2-5. Altocumulus is another sign of moist, unstable air aloft.

laws of physics say that it will become stable and that usually means the passage of a front to set things right.

One thing to remember is that alto clouds are middle clouds. If you fly under a bank of middle clouds from an area of what was better weather, then you can usually expect to encounter even lower clouds in your future. The decision process to continue or abort the flight needs to begin at this point. Certainly, altocumulus clouds will not force you to land at this point. They are warning signs, however, and you need to review your alternate plans. The altocumulus clouds, as you fly toward the deterioration, will become altostratus or overcast. Next, some stratus will slide below. In a few miles, possibly, rain will begin. If you aren't IFR rated, you shouldn't even be here. If you are, get on the radio and pick up a clearance. Keep in mind, though, that summer can be an exception to the trend toward lower and lower clouds.

Altostratus

In the previous section, we discussed how altocumulus clouds ahead of a warm front tend to become altostratus and so on down the line until the weather deteriorates completely. Altostratus can be found behind warm fronts in the warm sector (Fig. 1-1 for warm sector). If the low pressure system is moving northeastward along the jet stream, then it can be days into the future before the associated cold front moves through the area—if at all. This is when altostratus clouds can be almost nondescript as far as weather indicators. In other words, you can expect the present weather pattern to continue over 200 miles or more in just about any direction (Table 2-7, Fig. 2-6).

There is a possible danger, however, from this type of weather situation. It can breed contempt—and that is a dangerous thing in an airplane, my friend. Keep vigilance to the windward for an increase in clouds. It is possible for a lot of clouds to follow these pictured. The problem comes if it clears. You might expect to continue on without much problem. If the humidity is high, though, low stratus and scud will form, especially in coastal regions. That can make VFR flying at night unhandy to say the least.

Also during periods of altostratus cloud cover, you can expect the visibility to be down. As mentioned, humidity has a way of bringing low clouds and visibilities about. In the summer, visibilities may not be as bad, but the chance for thunderstorms in the warm sector exists.

Essentially, you can find all sorts of weather in a warm sector.

Table 2-7. Altostratus.

Trend	Component	Below 10,000'	Flight Time	Danger of	Possibly
No change	Wind	5-15 knots	Immediately	20-25 knots	Decreasing
Possible low clouds	Cloud	Scattered to broken low stratus	2-4 hours	low overcast to IFR minimums	Clearing
Little change	Pressure	Fall if nearing a cold front	3-4 hours	Fluctuations near TRWs	Rising
Moderately poor	Visibility	Possible haze layer	0-4 hours	Fog in drizzle	Improving
Usually drizzle	Precipitation	Should fly through quickly	1-4 hours	Thunderstorms	No rain or snow
Unseasonably warm	Temperature	Possible inversions	0-3 hours	Ice at highest winter	Continued hot watch CHT during taxis

It ranges from overcast low clouds and drizzle, thunderstorms, and mixed clouds at all altitudes to fair weather cumulus.

Stratus

Now we move into the lower clouds, stratus and cumulus. Both types can be associated with improving weather or deteriorating weather. The stratus in Fig. 2-7 photograph is the hallmark of imminent rain or snow. In this particular photo, it began to spit rain as I took the shot.

For the VFR pilot, overcast skies tend to be a detriment to safe flight if their bases are low. For the IFR flier, fuel required to make the trip must be planned accordingly. So overcast brings problems.

Fig. 2-6. Altostratus clouds mean the air aloft is stable. Continuous precip is possible, but heavy precip is unlikely.

Fig. 2-7. Low stratus and pannus. Pannus forms where it is raining.

If the bottoms are becoming ragged and dark gray bases can be observed, then you're in for a shower, almost immediately if not sooner. These shredded clouds indicate that precipitation is already falling (Table 2-8).

Figure 2-7 is the epitome of a warm front very close at hand. The conditions may persist for several days. They will possibly improve as the warm sector moves in or in the case of flight (IFR I might add) we move out into the sun and fair weather cumulus. Remember, warm fronts are often followed by cold fronts. This can translate into having to transition through two areas of inclement weather.

Table 2-8. Stratus and Pannus.

Component	Trend	Below 10,000′	Flight Time	Danger of	Possibly
Wind	Increase	20-30 knots at the surface	0-5 minutes	Windshear	Only small change
Cloud	Total cover of pannus	Layered some vertical develop- ment	0-2 hours	IFR ceiling	MVFR
Pressure	Falling		Next 4 hours	Extreme fall	Slow fall if depression weak or distant
Visibility	Decrease	Total obscuration at altitude 3 miles on landing	½ to 4 hours	½ mile in rain & fog	4-5 miles
Precipitation	Imminent	Through all altitudes	0-30 minutes	Heavy rain or snow showers	Light, inter- mittent showers
Temperature	Immediate fall	Possible freezing level within	0-30 minutes	Ice in clouds and precipitation	No ice

The clouds pictured in Fig. 2-7 can also be on the backside of a cold front. They are snowmakers of the most prominent type, so in wintertime watch for ice in clouds of this type and possibly heavy snow showers.

The inflight decision on whether to continue ahead or stop must be made *here*, if you are only VFR rated. If you are IFR equipped and rated, then you should already be on an IFR flight plan by this time. Possibly, you might already be plunging through the clouds above. To continue VFR past this point is to put yourself in a precarious position. Believe me, these clouds say that improvement will be a long while in coming. It's no time to be an optimist.

Cumulus or Cumulus Congestus

When we see clouds like this in flight, it may be too late to do much if you're only VFR rated. When Fig. 2-8 was taken I was in a holding pattern waiting for a massive thunderstorm to move off of the Wichita Falls airport. The storm was to the front, you might say, and the clouds pictured were guarding the rear. There were very few options at this point. If we had been eastbound (the direction pictured), IFR would be necessary. Cumulus mammatus clouds were at the high altitudes. This cloud type is shown at the top of Fig. 2-8. Ordinarily dark and bulbous, these clouds are seen at the top of the storms where the anvil top is just beginning to blow off. These clouds can also develop near the base of a storm, usually in advance of the rain shaft. Make no mistake, encountering these clouds at any altitude will be a rough experience (Table 2-9).

Fig. 2-8. Cumulus or cumulus congestus due to an upper air disturbance.

Table 2-9. Cumulus and Cumulus Congestus (Associated with Frontal Passage).

Component	Trend	Below 10,000'	Flight Time	Danger of	Possibly
Wind	Increase in vertical gusts	1-2,000 fpm updrafts	0-40 minutes	100 knots	35 knots or less
Cloud	Increase in vertical height	IFR necessary	0-40 minutes	Continuous cloud through 40,000' plus	Not much increase in height
Pressure	Falling		For the past hour, next 1 hour	Rapid fall near cells	No fall
Visibility	Remain good	Good out of clouds	0-1 hour	Zero in heavy rain	3-5 miles
Precipitation	Heavy, intermittent	Rain, hail	0-1 hour	Large hail	Light showers
Temperature	Cooler	5-10 degrees cooler	0-1 hour	Icing above 10,000'	No change

In the center of Fig. 2-8 is an area of clear sky. Around that area are piles of cumulus. These are in the growing stage. At the moment the picture was snapped, straight ahead was the only option for a VFR pilot to continue, and really not a very good one. IFR is really needed because the tops are going through 15,000 feet and getting higher by the minute.

In the lower portion of Fig. 2-8, fractostratus is prominent. Remember, whenever fractostratus is present, it is most generally formed by the close presence of precipitation. It is formed similarly to the stream formed from a warm shower in a cold bathroom. Believe me, if there are any airports in the immediate area, the VFR pilot should set the aircraft down and wait for the skies to clear.

Clouds or formations of clouds of this type don't just pop up for no reason. The thundery areas like this one occur in spring. This one happened in late spring when most of the storms were not building to serious proportions. Generally, an upper level trough or low pressure area causes the instability. Surface heating during the warm months causes thermals. Whenever an upper air disturbance moves over an area, then these thermals are encouraged to grow from their lower and middle air breeding grounds right up into the upper atmosphere.

Thundery weather like this will build up in the early afternoon (this picture was shot at 12:30 p.m.). Often it will pass through an area in less than an hour. However, an aircraft can travel many miles in an hour. If this weather situation lies ahead of you, a decision must be made. You may penetrate this area or sit and wait. The problem with waiting is that these storms may last till way after midnight due to their upper level support. If you are heading eastbound, it may become even longer before the trip can continue because of the eastward movement of the entire system. A good idea is to plan your trips early in the morning if at all possible and avoid heavy spring weather that pops up in the afternoon.

At 12:30 on this afternoon we were westbound. We deviated some 35 miles around a large cell. What would I have done if eastbound? I would have continued because flying is my profession and the weather pictured is penetrable with a good working radar—but not for long. The only stipulation is that IFR flight is a necessity from my point of view. The cloud bases are too low and the tops are too numerous and high to avoid. With good radar and help from the Air Route Center controller, a safe but somewhat bumpy flight is possible in the miles ahead. If you don't have the radar equipment or experience or both, it would be a great time to get a cup of coffee or a soft drink and wait for a rainbow.

Of course, we must all gain experience and build our personal limitations up through that experience. On this particular day, however, and even though I advocate being cautiously curious, this was not a system that an inexperienced pilot would easily handle. Possibly, a trial attempt on this day could prove disastrous, due to lack of options. Once a pilot was committed to a course of action, he was along for the ride no matter what.

Stratus and Stratocumulus

Cold fronts are known for their steep slopes—and that translates into fast-changing weather. The clouds in Fig. 2-9 are typical of those found near or in the immediate area of a cold front. The

Fig. 2-9. Stratus or stratocumulus. These clouds would be lying flat except for the lifting going on as this cold front approached.

Table 2-10. Stratus and Stratocumulus (Associated with Frontal Passage).

Component	Trend	Below 10,000'	Flight Time	Danger of	Possibly
Wind	Immediate shears and gusts	35-40 knots	0-30 minutes	20-30 knots horizontal shears	5-10 knots horizontal shears
Cloud	Bases lowering then raising	7/8 to 8/8 coverage	0-2 hours	Very low stratus w/ snow	Clearing rapidly with weak system
Pressure	Falling, then steady rise		0-30 minutes	Slow rise if weak	Little change
Visibility	Decrease	3 miles or less	0-2 hours	¼ mile in snow	Greater than 3 miles
Precipitation	Widespread showers, then bcmg scattered	Snow or rain depending on OAT.	0-4 hours	Wet snow or freezing drizzle	Little or none
Temperature	Falling	Inversions possible	0-30 minutes	Icing all altitudes	No ice early fall or late spring

clouds are definitely layered. It is very obvious nonetheless that these are clouds with substantial turbulence, and thus must have vertical extent, which throws them into the stratocumulus category.

Clouds of this type can often be observed with squall lines, as these were. However, these same sort of clouds can be predominant in late fall and early winter as the vanguard for snowy or blizzardous conditions. As we began this section, we mentioned their correlation to cold fronts. With clouds of this nature, expect a significant temperature drop. In winter, a significant temperature drop can mean icing conditions in precipitation or cloud, even when flying in the southern parts of the United States (Table 2-10).

From the standpoint of flying weather like this, IFR is the best choice. I must admit, though, taking off and flying into these clouds may give one his lumps. If these clouds are associated with thunderstorms, then forget it. However, if this is a cold front in late fall and snow or sleet is the only possible precipitation, then go ahead and fly it. I say this because experience has taught me that the turbulence is just not as bad in the winter.

One other thing—watch your outside air temperature gauge and check the corners of your windshield for ice to begin forming. When ice shows up, it's time to start looking for alternatives immediately. Usually those alternatives are to go up, down, or turn around. A good preflight briefing will give you an idea which is the best direction to go.

Towering Cumulus and Cumulonimbus

Early morning flying can be a time of beauty. In fact, it can produce an inspirational feeling where one feels a close kinship with his maker. Watching clouds like these grow seem to exhilarate a pilot. They are tremendous in size, as large or larger than any mountain in the Rockies. Growing quickly, they also spin the need for decisions.

The clouds, on the morning that I shot Fig. 2-10 over southern Oklahoma, were easy to avoid. They were associated with a low pressure trough, true enough, but it was quite early, near sunrise. As a result, they weren't taking the same form that they would in the afternoon.

In flying this type of weather, expect the clouds to become larger and more numerous the later in the day it becomes. You don't really want to fly through these little devils because they do have the capacity to shake you up. On occasion, however, penetrating a cloud such as this near its shoulder is necessary. I've even found it to be lots of fun. Be careful to "size up" the cloud carefully. Those that are 20,000 feet in height should be left alone. Those under 15,000 feet can be flown. Between 15,000 and 20,000 feet they become marginal as far as comfort and safety is concerned (Table 2-11).

One thing you can expect is some areas of showers. If you have radar it should be painting a few cells in the area. The cloud cover might be from 4/8 to 6/8. The showers will tend to grow most over areas of higher terrain. Another fine clue to the overall weather

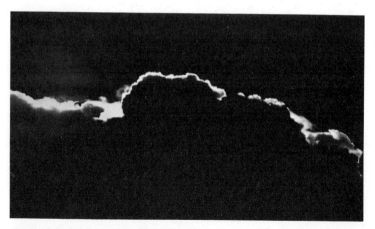

Fig. 2-10. Towering cumulus are the prelude to thundery weather. They are often mentioned in hourly sequence reports.

Table 2-11. Towering Cumulus and Cumulonimbus.

Component	Trend	Below 10,000'	Flight Time	Danger of	Possibly
Wind	Increasing in vicinity of RW's	20-30 knots	0-2 hours.	45 knot gusts	Little change
Cloud	Increasing	4/8-6/8 towering Cu	0-2 hours	Overcast cumulonimbus	Only towering cumulus
Pressure	Stable or rising slightly		0-2 hours	Rapid fall near large rain cells	No change
Visibility	Remain good	10-15 miles	0-2 hours	½ mile in rain	Decrease to average of 5 miles
Precipitation	Intermittent rain till middle evening	Moderate intensity	0-2 hours	Small hail	No rain
Temperature	Warm	Usual lapse rate	0-4 hours	10 degree drop near strong cells	Warming

picture is to note whether showers do develop. If they do not, then a major depression may be upwind. Check for cirrus and note the fallstreaks. Generally, clouds of this nature will not handicap your navigational efforts to a great extent.

Fog

The inland variety of fog that we will discuss here is often associated with warm fronts, but this is not always the case. Some of the worst fogs I have seen occurred during winter when there was snow on the ground. Both types are formed in the same manner—by warmer air moving over cooler ground or water.

The Great Lakes region is famous for fog in early winter before the lakes have frozen solid. Often the lakes and bays are quite cool—just above freezing. Air temperatures in the upper 30s to low 40s are prime fog-makers then. These fogs tend to be quite localized, rarely moving more than a mile or two inland from the water. Airports like Traverse City, Michigan, for example, are within a mile of East Grand Traverse Bay. The airport often goes down below IFR landing minimums until the fog abates.

In Oklahoma, where I am based, fogs form during winter as well. Snowy ground cover often produces fog so thick that prop blades will virtually cut corkscrew patterns in it. It is developed from the same conditions—warmer air over the cooler snow.

You may know already that temperature and dewpoint are related to cloud formation. In reality, fog *is* a cloud with low bases—*very* low! So as far as predicting fog, watch the difference in degrees between the temperature and dewpoint. Ordinarily, if they

Table 2-12. Fog.

Component	Trend	Below 10,000'	Flight Time	Danger of	Possibly
Wind	Little velocity	Air smooth	0-2 hours	No change to blow fog away	Light breeze
Cloud	Zero ceiling raising to low stratus or clear	Usually clear above fog deck	Fog can be very local	No change	Low stratus
Pressure	Usually high or rising slightly		0-2 hours	Dropping in advance of warm front	No change
Visibility	Low, but can be variable	Usually good above fog layer	0-2 hours	Zero	1-3 miles
Precipitation	Misty	Occasional drizzle	0-2 hours	Moderate rain near warm front	Only mist
Temperature	No change or warmer	Inversion on top of fog	0-2 hours	Warmer after fog lifts	No change

* 0-2 hours in the flight time indicate the amount of time it would take to transit through a warm front if these were the conditions on hand and fog was not local

are within four degrees of each other, fog is likely to form. There are exceptions. When the air is particularly dry and dust-free, fog may not form even if the temperature and dewpoint are the same. This phenomena is particularly prevalent in arid or semi-arid regions (Table 2-12).

Fog does have a bright side. Most mornings when you arrive to find the airplane shrouded in mist, you can fly anyway. As the temperature increases after sunrise, the fog will usually lift (Fig. 2-11). One thing that can happen is for the fog to lift in a layer and become a low stratus deck. When the weather does this, the fog may not completely burn away, leaving the VFR pilot stranded and the IFR pilot a deck to punch immediately after takeoff.

Fig. 2-11. Fog usually burns off before noon. This picture was taken at 7:30 a.m. and by 8:30 a.m. the sky was clear.

Well, there it is—about nine different looks that clouds take on. Of course, there are a myriad of varieties and combinations, but with these nine main looks, you should be able to develop a fair idea what each cloud type means when associated with the other factors. With long-term changes such as those that cirrus clouds predict, the most important supporting factor is probably the pressure. In clouds, such as cumulus that predict weather on the short term, visibility and wind direction should be given extra weight. Conditions of fog require you to give temperature the most consideration along with the dewpoint. These factors are important in understanding the conditions the clouds are predicting. Once you become familiar with each of the cloud types, it becomes much easier to place a cloud type with a particular type of weather pattern.

Chapter 3

Be Warm Front Wary

Almost any pilot flying is able to recognize a cold front. It's difficult to misinterpret the dark gray wall and bold audacity of this work of nature when it shakes the ground around you—not to mention the cold air and precip that follows from the North. Notwithstanding, recognition of the warm front might be one of the finer arts of piloting an aircraft. The problem with warm fronts is their hideousness. They have duped hundreds of pilots over the years into unsuspected terror.

One of the problems with warm fronts is their changeable nature. No two are ever exactly the same. The flight safety problems of warm fronts are either structural icing or imbedded thunderstorms. These two menaces almost never present themselves in a manner that makes a go or no-go decision easy. We've always been told to make a 180-degree turn and get the hell out. With warm fronts, recognizing when enough is enough is never clear-cut. As a result, the safe and careful airman must arm himself with some basic tools that will enable him/her to sort through the murk ahead and know when it's time to concede to Mother Nature.

Comparing cold fronts and warm fronts is like comparing apples and oranges. Cold fronts have steep frontal slopes and warm fronts have shallow ones. This is a most important reason why warm fronts are so hideous. It takes a long time to reach a point that intercepts the frontal slope at altitude. By that time it has been cloudy or possibly even raining or snowing for some time (Fig. 3-1).

Warm fronts are caused by warmer air overtaking and riding up

Fig. 3-1. Warm fronts cause widespread clouds, fog, and drizzle.

over the trailing edge of a mass of cooler air (Fig. 3-2). The shallow frontal slope that we just discussed causes widespread cloudiness and a trend toward low visibilities. The upshot of all this is quite a large area of bad weather that moves slowly. The only saving grace is that warm fronts are ordinarily much less severe than their cold-footed brothers.

Weather maps can give us clues as to what to expect. For example, imagine a low pressure system in northwestern Kansas. Then dangle a cold front down through the panhandle areas of Oklahoma and Texas. Extend it on out through far west Texas near El Paso. A typical warm front might then extend through central Kansas to southern Missouri and northern Tennessee. Remembering that low pressure systems circulate in a counterclockwise direction, we find we have a southwesterly flow south of the warm front. Cooler air is to the north of the warm front in southern Nebraska. Warm air persists in the warm sector (see Chapter 1) over central Kansas and northern Oklahoma. Relatively cold air is held back behind the cold front in Colorado and New Mexico.

As we discussed in Chapter 2, cirrus clouds are often the bearers of weather news. Cirrus clouds are always the vanguard of a warm front. They are found where the warm air is forced aloft to 20,000 feet or more. Because a warm front's slope is usually only one percent or less, cirrus clouds may be found as much as 500 miles or more in advance of the front itself. Of course there is a lot of good flying weather towards the front for many miles. There is no need to "shut her down," yet. One of the nice things about warm fronts is that the cloud sequence tells of their whereabouts. Approaching a warm front from the north, the clouds will appear in this sequence:

43

cirrus, cirrostratus, altostratus, and nimbostratus with imbedded cumulonimbus. Precipitation may start about 300 miles in advance of the front.

The warm sector is the wedge of air south of the warm front. The weather is likely to improve in that area but there's no assurance it will. The wind direction north of the front is generally east or southeast. South, in the warm sector, the wind shifts around to the southwest which usually brings in drier air. If the air is moist and unstable there is the continuing chance of more showers and low visibilities. This is an inversion-type effect and cloud tops are usually low.

Two Sides of the Coin

As with coins, there are two sides to every front. They are as different as heads and tails. Approaching the front from the southwest, a VFR pilot would not be likely to continue the flight. The clouds are tall from low bases and actually form a wall of dark gray similar to facing a cold front from the south side. The no-go decision is easy here. The clouds look too menacing.

From the north side, however, a VFR pilot flying from good weather to the north may be tempted to continue because the situation looks far from difficult or ominous. Optimistically, the VFR pilot will continue. Eventually, though, rain starts to fall from the altostratus—light rain at first, not very restrictive to inflight visibility. The visibility may hold for a while, but essentially you can believe that once the rain starts, conditions will continue to de-

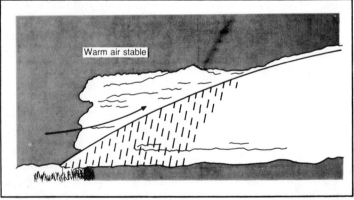

Fig. 3-2. A cross-section of a warm front with overrunning moist, stable air. The clouds that result are stratiform and widespread. The precip is continuous and induces lower stratus in the cold air.

teriorate. Continuing to fly in the face of gathering warning signals will eventually put the VFR pilot in serious trouble.

If the weather has forced the VFR pilot to sit it out, there is little to do but wait. The thing to look for is not necessarily the sky to clear, but rather, evidence that it will. This is where weather knowledge shows its worth and you can make a prediction on your own. The major inference that you are looking for is a wind shift. On the backside of warm fronts, ordinarily the south side, the wind moves around to the southwest. The temperature should also rise a few degrees. When this happens, the skies may begin to clear. If the flying weather is to be good, you should observe the main clouds fractionating, followed by fair weather cumulus. Remember, cold fronts follow warm fronts, often by hours. If the destination is not much farther up the road, say 100 to 150 miles or so, the weather should improve for the whole trip.

The instrument-rated pilot has more options than the VFR pilot. In fact, the IFR pilot may make another 100 to 150 miles in the same direction as the VFR pilot before he would have to call it quits. In some cases, the IFR pilot may not have to quit at all. The danger or risk to the IFR pilot is two-fold. First, there may be imbedded thunderstorms. Secondly, low visibility due to fog may cause a missed approach at the destination. Although warm front variety thunderstorms are the least severe of thunderstorm types under normal conditions, any TRW can bend a plane into odd and diverse shapes, so your thunderstorm experience can play a very large part in your decision to fly into the warm frontal area.

The private pilot or business pilot sometimes may elect not to fly on toward the destination whenever below IFR minimums are forecast. This is probably a good choice if a closer destination (alternate) will not suffice. The point is, why push it? The destination is what is needed, not the alternate. The ideal way to handle it is to wait for some improvement. How long you will have to wait depends upon the personality of the warm front.

There are techniques for determining the personality of a warm front. These clues come from your ability to understand and comprehend cloud formations. For example, if you are expecting a warm front in your direction of flight, you should begin immediately after takeoff to note the cloud type you encounter. If cirrocumulus clouds are encountered first, it's a strong bet that the overriding warm air is plenty moist and unstable. Bear in mind that cumulus clouds always indicate some amount of instability. Whenever cirrocumulus is the leading cloud type, expect thunderstorms in the frontal area. Cirrocumulus clouds are those that often form the "mackerel sky" and sailors know that a gale is in the offing.

On the other hand, the leading clouds of a warm front may be strictly cirrus, blending into cirrostratus and then altostratus. This means, as you may have already figured, stable air. At this point it may be possible to characterize the front as stable and dry. It may be that the only way you would know of frontal passage or penetration through the front would be by a wind shift and slight temperature rise. If you are airborne, you can figure on a course correction to the right as with all fronts, warm or cold, a rise on the OAT gauge, and a slight rise in the barometric pressure or altimeter setting. All of those things are handy and tend to be very good forecasting tools.

Since the seasons change, the classic warm front may take on added complications in the cold months. In mid-winter, regardless of geographic locale, icing of the airframe becomes an important problem. You can expect rime ice in most warm fronts due to the stratiform clouds. However, as the aircraft flies nearer to the frontal zone, you may encounter cumuliform types of clouds. It may be impossible to tell what type of cloud you are flying in when it is solid instruments, but that mixed or even clear ice that builds so fast is enough to tell the tale. In far northern areas of the United States (in what is generally considered the "snow belt"), temperatures at ground level may be well below freezing. The cumuliform clouds above, then, may carry ice all the way to the top. For us little guys, the choice becomes obvious—land!

One other important point about icing in warm fronts. Occasionally there is an inversion that can be topped by an aircraft near the front. Actually, it is not an inversion but the front itself. Since warm fronts can cause widespread precipitation and some of it originates above this warmer level of the front, airframe icing from precipitation is highly likely. In some instances, you can climb and reach an altitude that is above the freezing level, and be safe to complete the trip. This will only work when front is close at hand for unpressurized aircraft. Icing from precipitation is often quick to build up and very dangerous. Don't take longer than a few seconds to begin looking for a way out.

The Blizzard Builder

A low during the winter months can be an incredible blizzard builder. It happens when the anticyclonic winds reach down south and bring warm moist air up and over the cold air and push it around to the north side. The warm moist air eventually cools to its dewpoint as it is lifted even higher. Finally, too heavy from its water content and too cool anymore to stay in cloud, it drops out. Falling thousands of feet into the cooler—even cold—air below, it changes from rain to snow. This snow, like the drizzle in summer, associated with warm fronts, may occur 300 to 400 miles in advance of the front. The result is usually wet snow covering a huge portion of the country in a white swath.

For the aviator, a blizzard is no place to go or to want to go. The term *blizzard* implies blowing snow and possible heavy snow showers. These conditions, and the highly likely possibility of structural icing, require a no-go decision. Believe me, even the major air carriers will be cancelling.

You may have noticed (if you are a weather watcher, as I am), that warm fronts rarely move as fast as cold fronts. The reason for this is that cold fronts have huge high pressure pumps forcing the cold air south and east. This makes them more powerful, quicker-moving, and affecting a given area for a shorter period of time. The trouble with all this is that the cold front may catch the warm front, causing a confusing mess know as an *occluded front*. From the north side, the cloud sequence remains the same as for a warm front. The warm moist air of the warm front, however, is hoisted aloft and becomes undercut from the backside by the cold front. At that point the pre-warm-frontal cloud sequence will be indistinguishable from that of a cold front and there is a metamorphosis. Occluded fronts are strong. As a matter of fact, the frontal system is strongest along the occlusion. As a result, the weather conditions are more severe than either a warm or cold front. There will be more heavy precipitation, higher winds, and lower clouds. This type of weather system is most predominant in the upper Midwest and East Coast of the country. If this is your hunting grounds, watch for it in the winter. You probably won't want to leave the comfort of your home.

Regardless of the time of year, the warm front can cloud the minds of even the most experienced fliers with uncertainty. When discussing weather, every rule has an exception. This is what makes flying such a challenge and a rewarding experience apart from the exhilaration of flight. Every pilot owes it to himself and his passengers to equip himself with all the knowledge about weather possible. It is the stuff of which great flights and happy endings are made.

Chapter 4
Cold Fronts
and Other Frontal Weather

Every front has its own personality. We have already talked about warm fronts. Now we will discuss the cold front and the various phases it can go through. All this tends to give the weatherwise pilot more options by knowing what future conditions may be.

All cold fronts have a source region. As they move out of their regions, they move into contact with other air masses that have different properties. This zone between two different and sometimes opposing air masses is called a *front*. Whenever the properties of two air masses differ greatly, the change can be quite abrupt. The properties of which we speak are temperature, humidity, and wind. When the change is abrupt, the frontal zone is narrow. This is usually the case with cold fronts as opposed to the broader warm fronts.

Temperature, of course, is the most recognizable characteristic across most cold fronts. This might not always hold true with summer cold fronts because of their weak intensity. Dewpoint can be extremely helpful when sizing up a cold front (or any front for that matter). Dewpoint tends to give information about the differences of cloudiness to be expected. The idea here is to check reporting stations ahead and behind the front for their dewpoints to get a feel for how much moisture is caught up in the system. The closer the temp and dew point, the more likely clouds will tend to form at a low level.

Wind always changes across a front. The direction it takes directly behind a cold front is an indicator of its intensity. For example, most weak fronts tend to display a northeasterly direction within a few hours after frontal passage. This usually means or can mean that the front is losing its punch and may become stationary or diffuse. When the winds remain strong for some time behind the front from a northwesterly direction, there is a strong frontal system and a large high pressure system propelling it.

The other property that changes across a front is pressure. Pressure is generally in cold air. As a result, expect an abrupt rise in your altimeter setting after passing the front. Because all flights do not cross a front at an angle perpendicular to the front, even a strong front may not exhibit a quick change. The important thing to keep in mind is that the rate-of-change in barometric pressure will change.

In Fig. 4-1 we have the cross-section of a cold front. At the surface, cold air is overtaking and replacing warmer air. Compare

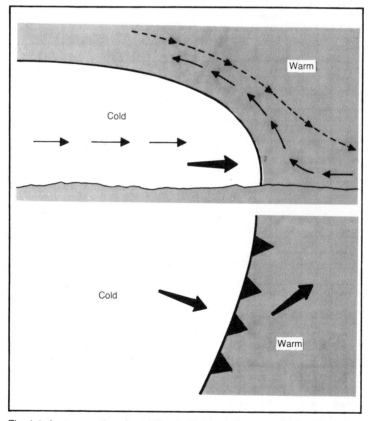

Fig. 4-1. A cross-section of a cold front with its weather map presentation below it. The arrows indicate the various air movements.

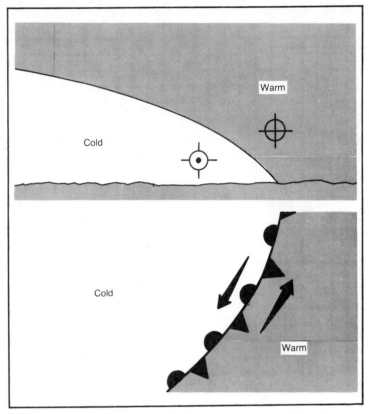

Fig. 4-2. Cross-section of a stationary front and its associated weather map below it. The arrows represent the air movement about the front.

this illustration with Fig. 3-2 for the warm front in the previous chapter. You can see that there is much difference in the gradient of their frontal slopes. If you have ever wondered how fast a particular front is moving, there is a way to find out. As we discussed in Chapter 1, the wind (represented by isobars on a surface map) tends to flow very nearly perpendicular across the frontal zone. When getting a preflight briefing, a check of the lowest winds aloft forecast from a point just ahead of the front will be equal to its rate of movement.

When the properties of two air masses start to become nearly alike, the rate of movement and hence the difference in wind velocity between the two become negligible. Neither air mass is replacing the other. This condition is known as a *stationary front* (Fig. 4-2). In this case, surface winds begin to blow parallel to the front. The slope of a stationary is usually shallow. It may be steep, nevertheless, if the density between the two air masses is quite different.

Life Cycle of a Frontal Wave

Flying cold fronts is so much easier if you have an understanding of the big picture. What I call the "big picture" is knowing where the low pressure areas lie and how the fronts are draped from them. By knowing some of the characteristics of cold fronts you can, to some extent, predict the weather ahead. Often, flying along, watching the weather through the windshield, is the best place to observe the current trend. It actually is so much better than the ground observer's position that a pilot can often forecast a change hours ahead of the Weather Service. This is chiefly because the airplane is exposed to a cross-section of the big picture and the people on the ground use only their observations and those of others miles away. Because of this one fact, the importance of the big picture cannot be discounted.

When we check the weather from a Flight Service briefer he usually gives us observations from various points such as, "Kansas City, 1,500 overcast, two miles and fog. Omaha is reporting measured 500 overcast, one mile, light snow and fog." When this is the only information that you request, you cheat yourself and stack the cards against your favor. The reason for this should be plain: The weather between Kansas City and Omaha is unknown. Is the snow condition at Omaha some sort of local condition or is there a front in the area? Knowledge of the big picture can dispel a great deal of doubt in your mind.

As a matter of interest, or even as a hobby, I continually watch the weather programs on television. As an airline pilot, it's plenty important to know where all the little ripples are in the overall picture. And it should be for you too, whether you fly daily or not. By knowing the average life cycle of a front it may become possible for almost any pilot to get a feel for what the weather will do next. Sure, there are times when we will all be wrong, but a lot of times you may be right when the weather service isn't.

In the next few paragraphs, we will be referring to part A of Fig. 4-3 on the life cycle of a frontal wave. The pointed barbs represent the direction of movement of the cold air and the rounded spades represent the movement of the warm air.

Figure 4-3A can be likened to the conception of a living thing. At this point it is only a twinkle in the weatherman's eye. Here the winds are blowing in opposite directions but parallel to the developing front. This sort of condition occurs between a low and high pressure system. As the air masses grow more in contrast to each other, the identity of the cold and warm air becomes apparent. The barometric pressure changes across the front. The dewpoints begin to become obverse. The process we are watching is *frontogenesis*. As the barometric differential begins to increase, the front begins to ripple. The wave has begun to form. The beginning of the wave is shown in Fig. 4-3B. It is apparent at this time where the center of low pressure will be. Essentially, a pivotal point around which the fronts will move is forming.

The front reaches its adolescent stage, shown at Fig. 4-3C,

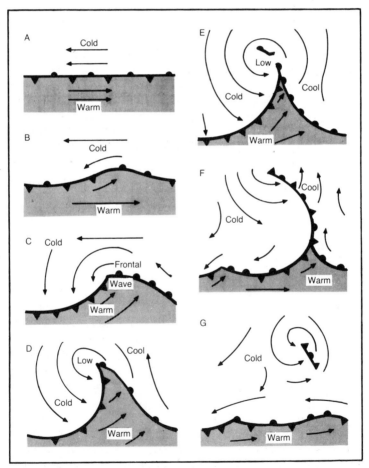

Fig. 4-3. The life cycle of a frontal wave.

with cyclonic circulation well established. At this time, weather forecasters are showing a low pressure system on their map. (It is interesting to note how the sequence of pictures resembles an ocean swell.)

Also in Fig. 4-3C it is apparent that the fronts have grown to have very separate identities. The warm front is being circulated northward and the cold front is being pushed to the south. The area to the south of both fronts, once again, is the warm sector. Moisture is greatest in this area. In the United States, moisture is generally pumped into a system from the Gulf of Mexico. This moisture usually affects the central part of the country. The East Coast often gets a mix of Gulf and Atlantic moisture, whereas, the West Coast receives the wet stuff from the Pacific.

As we have already discussed, moisture is being lifted as it approaches both fronts. The lifting is more defined or extreme over the cold front. As a result, the cold front produces more inclement and violent weather than its warmer brother. Moisture, being affected by gravity as is everything else, will eventually be precipitated. This is the main reason that you can expect precipitation near a front. The type of precipitation, I'm sure you realize, depends on the type of front and time of year as well as geographical location.

In Fig. 4-3D, the cyclone has grown to full adult strength. The winds just above the friction layer are now strong enough to cause the fronts to begin to move. As we discussed in the warm front chapter, the cold front moves faster than the warm front. In well-developed systems, it is not unusual for the cold front to move much faster than the warm front and result in an occlusion. This is significant because when the storm occludes, it has reached its maximum intensity as shown in Fig. 4-3E. This is probably the worst time to venture a trip through the fronts.

As a storm system reaches its most intense form with an occlusion (Figs. 4-4, 4-5), it also begins to weaken. As the occlusion grows in length from the low pressure center, the cyclonic circulation diminishes. Another disordered cold front may begin to form west of the occlusion as in Fig. 4-3F, but probably the two fronts may slow down and become a stationary front as in Fig. 4-3G. The occlusion remnant will eventually disappear and the air masses will begin to equalize on both sides of the front.

I am a proponent of watching the big picture. By doing so, it is possible to plan your trips days in advance. It is much more important to know or beware of the trends than to know the terminal forecasts for every point along the route of flight. Of course, check-

Fig. 4-4. When a warm and cold front meet, it is called an occlusion. This is a warm front occlusion. All types of weather associated with both types of fronts are present.

ing the terminal forecast before flight is recommended procedure. Terminal forecasts can be used to doublecheck the "big picture" or to identify local disturbances.

I have told this story before, but it is so indicative or demonstrative of cold fronts and the big picture that I feel compelled to tell it again. In preparing for a return trip from Cleveland to Traverse City, Michigan, I switched on the television to catch the evening weather program. The meteorologist had a strong cold front stretched from Northwestern Ontario down through the Cleveland area. The front was forecasted to move on by early the next morning. Reports from behind the front indicated a rapid clearing trend. The moderate-to-heavy snows we had been receiv-

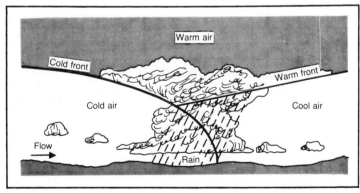

Fig. 4-5. A cold front occlusion is weather at its worst. In this example, warm, moist, stable air has been lifted aloft.

ing in the Cleveland area would abate. Having watched the progress of the front for the past several days, it was apparent that it was reaching its mature stage. The warm front to the north and east in Ontario had not yet been caught by its colder counterpart. They would probably occlude the following day, but that would be east of Cleveland and we would be spared. It would be an advantageous time to head north.

The next morning, in anticipation of the flight, I tuned in the *Today Show*. The prog charts that they show every morning represent the positions of systems for 12:00 noon Eastern Time. Sure enough, they had the front southeast of Cleveland and occluding at a point north of Buffalo, New York. Since there were no successive fronts close behind, the trip to northern Michigan appeared clear.

A call to Flight Service confirmed that the trip should be uneventful with the exception of our destination. Traverse City was forecasting scattered snow showers. Having a very good idea of the general position of all the fronts in the Midwest, I became interested in the cause of the snow showers. Further examination showed it to be a local condition only. Traverse City, you see, sits on two large bays near Lake Michigan. The snow that day was being produced by lake effect (Fig. 4-6).

Well, the trip was relatively uneventful, although terribly bumpy in the disturbed air behind the front. This anecdote, nevertheless, should demonstrate the value of knowing the general positions of fronts and how to plan ahead for your trip.

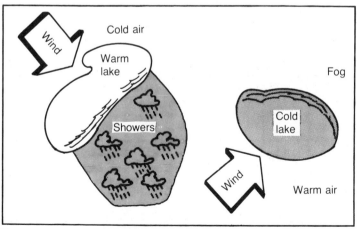

Fig. 4-6. Lake effect. Air moving over a sizable lake absorbs water vapor. The result can be showers on the leeward side if the air is colder than the water. When the air is warmer than the water, fog can develop.

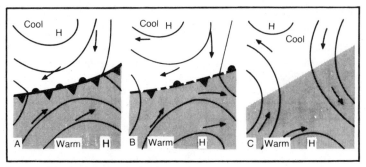

Fig. 4-7. The frontolysis of a stationary front.

Frontolysis and Frontogenesis

We just talked about the life cycle of a frontal wave. We mentioned how they form and how they dissipate. This is called *frontogenesis* and *frontolysis*, respectively.

Frontolysis is instigated as adjacent air masses modify and temperature and pressure differences equalize across the front. The front then dissipates in a fashion shown in Fig. 4-7.

Personalities of Cold Fronts

Each cold front has its own personal identity. These characteristics are brought on by factors we have already touched on such as temperature, pressure, dewpoint, and upper and lower wind directions and velocities. Now let's consider a few fronts with the aid of some illustrations.

In flying fronts, the weather varies from virtually clear skies to extreme hazards such as hail, turbulence, icing, low clouds, and poor visibilities. Basically, the weather occurring along a cold front is dependent upon the amount of moisture available, the stability of the air that is forced upward, the speed of the front, the slope, and finally, the upper wind flow.

To make flying difficult (or at least more difficult than on a clear day), a front must possess clouds. There simply has to be enough moisture or clouds will not form. Fronts without clouds are considered inactive. Inactive fronts can be very active in a short distance if they run into an area of moisture. This sort of thing happens often as a dry front comes from out of the Rockies onto the plains. Awaiting the front often is a tongue of moist air from the Gulf of Mexico. Thunderstorms may build quite rapidly and catch a pilot with his guard down.

The degree of instability of the lifted air determines which cloud type will form, stratiform or cumuliform. Of course, unstable air breeds cumuliform clouds and stable air generates the stratiform type. Precipitation from stratus clouds is generally steady and of only moderate intensity at best. The ride through these clouds is smooth. Precipitation from cumuliform clouds tends to be intermittent and showery and often heavy in intensity.

Shallow frontal surfaces tend to be extensive in area as are warm fronts. Cold fronts can also fall into this category. If the temperature of the cold air near the surface is below freezing but the air being lifted aloft is above freezing, the precip will fall as freezing rain or ice pellets. If the warmer air being hoisted aloft is below freezing itself, then snow will be the result.

Now let's look at various types of cold fronts. A cold front that underruns warm, moist, stable air will tend to have stratiform clouds and precipitation. Further precipitation will induce even more stratus to form in the cold air as shown in Fig. 4-8. This sort of front is more common in mid-winter after much of the significant temperature differences between air masses has been eradicated by many preceding cold fronts.

The cold fronts of early and middle fall are often fast-moving and tend to pack a wallop as far as precipitation is concerned. These fronts are likely to be underrunning warm, moist, unstable air (Fig. 4-9). Clouds are cumuliform with possible showers or thunderstorms near the surface position of the front. Convective clouds often form out ahead of the front and squall lines are a real possibility. The warm, wet ground behind the frontal system tends to generate low-level fair weather cumulus in the cold air. Flying this type of cold front is often the most difficult flying there is. Many

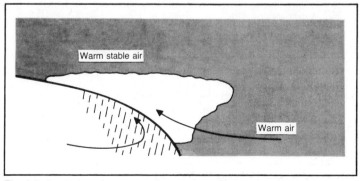

Fig. 4-8. A cold front is shown here underrunning warm, moist, stable air. The clouds are stratified and the precip is continuous. The warm rain causes stratus to form in the cold air behind the front.

Fig. 4-9. This cold front is undercutting warm, moist, unstable air. Thunderstorms are possible near the front.

times it is impossible to penetrate the frontal area even with radar because of the close proximity of the storms to each other—sort of the solid wall concept. On the bright side, the weather clears up rather quickly for a continuation of the trip once the front has passed.

Slow-moving cold fronts can occur any time of the year. Typically, we find these awful fellows in late summer or early fall. The frontal slopes are more shallow than a fast-mover and that usually means widespread weather or clouds (Fig. 4-10). When this type of system is lifting moist, warm, unstable air, the flying becomes quite

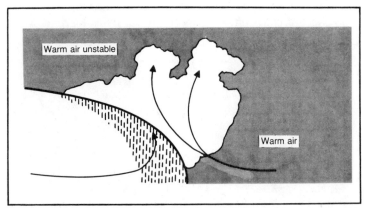

Fig. 4-10. This is a slow-moving cold front. It is undercutting warm, moist, unstable air. The frontal slope is more shallow than the front in Fig. 4-9. The clouds with a front such as this tend to be stratified with imbedded thunderstorms.

hazardous due to the imbedded aspect of individual cells. Airborne radar is almost a necessity.

The fast-moving variety of above cold front is not much easier to fly. The one saving grace of a fast-mover is that the convective clouds will be found only along the surface position of the front. This weather can be severe, but normally not as wide a disturbance as a slow-moving cold front.

Instability Line

There are lines of demarcation between air masses at times that cannot properly be called fronts. An *instability line* is one such phenomena. Usually, an instability line is a narrow band of convective activity. If the line develops fully into a line of thunderstorms, it is then called a *squall line*.

Instability lines form in moist unstable air. An instability line is a possibility far from any front, but more often than not, it forms in advance of fast-moving cold fronts. Even series of these lines have been known to develop. The terrible storm that spawned the Wichita Falls tornado of April 1979 was in the first of three lines of storms that moved through that city and adjacent communities. Residing in southwestern Oklahoma, I have witnessed this several times, where the television radar had several waves of heavy activity depicted.

Dewpoint fronts or dry lines are other good places for instability lines to form, which brings us to our next subject.

Dewpoint Front or Dry Line

During the spring and early summer dry lines are common in western Oklahoma, Texas, and New Mexico and northward over the Great Plains. These dry lines are caused by moist air moving north from the Gulf of Mexico. This air runs up against dryer air from the semi-arid regions of the three states we just mentioned. The dryer air has less moisture and is therefore more dense. Except for the moisture differences, there is seldom any air mass contrast across the line. Hence the name "dry line."

The weather conditions associated with dry lines can be docile or wild. Nighttime and early morning fog and low-level clouds are the standard on the moist south side of the front. Clear skies are the rule on the north side of the line. The trouble begins, though, in late afternoon when an instability line begins to form. Thunderstorms of the greatest proportions build to almost unheard-of levels. Some near Gage, Oklahoma, were measured by radar at the Severe

Storms Lab in Norman, Oklahoma, at 70,000 feet! Needless to say, watch out for this condition over the southwestern plains in springtime.

I guess it cannot be stressed enough that the big picture is the key to success in flying cross-country. You have an incomparable position from which to observe changing weather conditions. Taking some of what we have discussed so far in this book into the cockpit can make long flights as easy to complete as most of the short ones. Knowing the big picture makes it easy for you to choose alternate routes if the path to your destination becomes unworthy of further pursuit. In flying, you need two qualities especially: First, *be observant*. Second, *be flexible* in your planning. With these two attributes, any pilot can safely build up a storehouse of weather knowledge and flying experience to compare with the best.

Chapter 5

Getting the Most
from All Forecast Sources

It's six o'clock in the morning. The sun has not begun to make its daily appearance. From the looks of the snowflakes swirling around the corners of the window, it may not. The prospects of flying out of the local airfield this morning are as bleak as the driving snow. The runways, if you can find them, are probably covered with four or five inches of the white stuff. If your plane is tied down outside, an incredible ice and snow clearing job await you. Being IFR rated this day may make the difference in going at all. Snow clouds, being what they are, however, may be full of ice and no rating may be of much use. The questions are obvious to a pilot of any rating and experience! Will I be able to fly today or in the very near future? If not, will I be able to fly tomorrow? The answers to these questions lie with the pilot-in-command himself. It is necessary, nonetheless, to have facts upon which to base a decision.

Three basic avenues are available to you when considering a flight. One, you can call the Flight Service Station and contact a weather briefing specialist. Two, you can make weather observations on your own. Three, you can rely on a weather briefing specialist of another sort. This specialist is the meteorologist on television. Now, the Federal Aviation Regulations state that we pilots must receive an official weather briefing before each flight. This must come from either an FSS or the National Weather Service. Nowadays, it is rare for most pilots to have direct contact with the Weather Service. The main idea, though, is for the FAA to keep tabs on us to see if we did our homework prior to the flight if we become unfortunate enough to have an accident, weather-related or not. Essentially, what I am saying is that only *one* of the three avenues we have for weather information is required.

Forecasting by TV

Just because this FSS type of weather briefing is required by law, most pilots believe it is the best—or possibly they forget they have other information literally right before their eyes. The television can be a powerful tool when used to your advantage. I will admit, there are a great many "Mickey Mouse" local weather programs on the airways today. In recent years, though, most TV stations have made great inroads in this area. This is due to two main reasons. First, a number of highly educated meteorologists have been acquired by local station managements. Secondly, technology has brought us the "Laserfax" machine for reproducing in, large scale, photographs of the earth's cloud formations taken from satellites in space. When a station combines these two factors, success can be spelled in capital letters. The public is better informed and, believe it or not, better entertained. As you can imagine, that translates into more dollars for the station and justifies the salaries and equipment.

There are two other excellent television weather resources that you may have available, depending on your area. The first is the 24-hour Weather Channel, which provides aviation weather hourly. Originating in Atlanta, GA, The Weather Channel is available only by cable (or with a home satellite Earth station; it comes off SATCOM IIIR). The second resource is *A.M. Weather*, a 15-minute broadcast produced by the Maryland Center for Public Broadcasting and fed via satellite to over 250 Public Broadcasting System stations around the country. In its home state of Maryland, it's broadcast at 6:45 a.m. and updated at 8:45 a.m.; check your local listings for availability and time in your area. Pilots constitute a major portion of *A.M. Weather's* audience, and the data provided include turbulence, winds aloft at 2,000, 10,000, 18,000, and 34,000 (39,000 in summer) feet, and IFR and VFR aviation charts.

The question has now probably crossed your mind, "So are you going to tell me how to take advantage of all this magic?" Indeed, that time is upon us. All television weather programs are basically the same as far as format goes. Only the order in which the information is presented varies. Most programs present these items: position of all lows and highs and fronts (be they warm or cold) on a national map; local view of the present position of highs, lows, and fronts; prognosis of weather progression both national and local (local meaning state or states); present conditions locally; satellite picture; and finally, radar returns.

The main emphasis of most local programs is on the local or state picture. Although this can be very helpful on some flights, you as a pilot should probably dwell more on the national picture and prognosis. Where the local and state picture may suffice for a student on his first solo cross-country flight, the corporate or airline pilot flies out of this range almost daily. There will be times when even the student may have to venture outside the scope of this "station emphasized" area. The solution is to pay particular attention to the bigger picture. After all, it can be applied on the smallest of scales too, can it not?

So, obviously, the most important thing to you is the overall state of the atmosphere on the national map. Then what do you look for? If it is presented by the station you are watching, the jet stream is most important. As a general rule, the fronts and lows will move along and parallel to these upper level "steering" winds. By knowing the forecasted trail of the jet stream, you can therefore propose for yourself which direction a particular front or low pressure system will tend to travel. Obviously, you will pick out those weather features that are closest to your route of flight. Why not let the weatherman tell you which way the systems are going to move? For one reason, if you just let him spoon-feed you, you will tend to retain the information a shorter period of time. It is always better to have a full understanding of the mechanics of a problem to fully utilize the information gained from it. And who can't admire a pilot who is weather-wise?

Along with the jet stream, you should be able to pick up the position of the fronts and pressure systems. It is of the greatest importance that you have the present position of the systems, pertinent to your flight, firmly fixed in your mind. The importance of this point cannot be over emphasized. Without a starting point from which to work, you can never prognosticate the future. In plain terms, it would be possible to turn towards worsening weather if an alternate action was required in flight instead of towards improving weather. Rule Number One is *know where VFR weather is likely to be found*. This would apply if you are VFR rated and searching for VFR weather or IFR rated with a power failure looking for VFR weather.

Next in priority is the satellite picture. These have been the biggest boon to weather forecasting since God made the cloud. With all the reporting stations available to us, it is still thousands of times easier to understand the big picture when we can actually look at it. There is an art to looking at one of these stellar viewpoints. As we know as aviators, clouds have depth or height depending on our viewpoint. Low clouds of the stratus or especially the stratocumulus and cumulus types show up the least on the satellite picture. As a result, an area that appears clear may have marginal weather. If this cloudiness is widespread, the weatherman may point it out and direct our attention to it. Cirrus types show up the best. Simply because of their relative closeness to the camera they are more prominent.

As we mentioned earlier, thickness of cloud is not very well depicted on the two-dimensional picture on the tube. Experience has shown me a couple of ways to discern where thick cloud formations lie. Often the thinner cloud formation areas have breaks in them. If you can see Mother Earth anywhere through the clouds, it is a safe bet that the clouds do not go from surface up to these higher clouds anywhere in the near vicinity (about 100 to 150 miles). The cloud formations that are thick in appearance are usually behind a front. More often than not, these are associated with thunderstorm activity. In the winter, however, these may not be present. Also, these thunderstorms bear an extremely close resemblance to a cotton ball's texture. The whiteness is near the same, which adds an additional clue to the thickness of cloud in that particular area.

Winter clouds pose a slightly different problem. Rarely in winter do the clouds build to the proportions of those of summer. Granted, there are cirrus clouds up in the higher flight levels, but as mentioned earlier these do not have the density of thunderstorms. As a result, I have noticed that many times the winter cloud systems have a less white appearance, indicating that they are not as thick.

Often, the photos from space are taken at night; those on the 10 and 11 o'clock weather editions were probably taken in the neighborhood of 9 o'clock. These pictures are usually shot with infrared lenses. The resolution between black and white is therefore not as great. It is a common practice by television stations to enhance these photos by computer. When they do this, the coldest areas of cloud show up as black splotches. These colder clouds are generally the ones that are producing precipitation, and hence the thickest. If I haven't mentioned the importance of knowing the thickness of the clouds, it is that the thicker the clouds are in an area, the more that area is possibly affected by marginal weather (i.e., low ceilings and visibility).

When the satellite photo is used in tandem with the information on the jet stream, you have a very useful tool. Not all low pressure systems, for example, are wet (have cloud). The ones that *are* wet show up on the satellite. Frequently, the anticlockwise spiral of the wet low pressure system is quite evident on the photos. If you know the projected movement of that system due to knowing the steering winds, you can overlay in your mind, so to speak, where the clouds will lie at a particular time. Some stations have an overlay of the jet stream right on their satellite photos, and most stations have the fronts drawn on them as well. This makes your job very simple and aids greatly in your understanding.

The advent of radar into aviation is one of the reasons we get the utility out of our present day aircraft that we do. You don't have to be rich to enjoy the benefits of radar. Looking at storm returns on the television screen before leaving for the airport can provide priceless information. Unless there is an FSS with a radar unit of some type on the field that you fly out of, the TV radar may be the only one you ever get to look at. Sometimes, what you see may make you cancel the trip or postpone it for a while. The great benefit, however, is using it to decide how best to circumnavigate the weather. There are times when the radar information that you get from Flight Service is so old that it is not representative of the situation at all. If it is the time of day that a TV radar picture is broadcast, you can have an up-to-the-second idea of the weather and precip pattern.

One of the items of a regular weather broadcast on television is the listing of present conditions. Commonly, these are temperature, dewpoint or humidity, wind direction and velocity, barometric pressure and trend, and the general cloud cover. Just having a knowledge of these factors can be enough to alert a weather-wise pilot to upcoming changes in the local pattern. It is easy to recognize signs of changing weather when you know what to look for. Let's discuss the important points.

Barometric pressure and its trend is the most easily understood method for predicting a change. It is far from foolproof, though. Almost anyone knows that when the pressure is falling, the weather is probably deteriorating. On a large scale this is true. The trouble with this is that the atmosphere is full of small burbles and the barometric pressure may change up or down depending on such things as high altitude systems passing over an area or intense differential heating of the neighboring countryside. As an observer of the weather pattern, then, you are left to decide which excursions from normal are representative of weather to come. Of course, you can relate barometric trends to the big picture, but pushing that aside there is a way to recognize changes without knowing the overall weather pattern of the nation. The key is "it takes patience." Watching reports for at least 24 hours should be enough for you to notice the true barometric trend. Simply put, if it is falling, there is an approaching low pressure center. If it is rising, there is an approaching high pressure center. As we discussed in the very first chapter of this book, high pressure does not automatically mean good weather, nor does low pressure mean bad weather. Unfortunately, the barometric trend will not give all the necessary clues to the future.

It becomes evident, then, that if the barometric pressure is not enough to serve the purpose, there must be some other handy clues. Temperature is one of them. As a general rule, southerly winds precede all fronts. The air mass arriving from the south, unsurprisingly, is usually warm. Often it is warmer than the front that last moved through an area. The temperature trend before a front—*any* kind of front—is a warming trend. Warm fronts bring warm air northward fairly gradually. Then, as the front nears or passes a locality, the temperature usually rises several degrees quite rapidly. This air is known as the *warm sector*, of which we have spoken several times already.

Warm sectors inevitably precede cold fronts. The air mass temperature in these wedges between the warm front to the north-east and the cold front to the northwest can be very homogenous. Still, the air flowing into this sector is driven by a southerly wind and some sort of a warming trend will ensue. The point we are trying to make is that if the temperature is rising somewhat, a front may be in the offing. Couple the temperature observation with the barometric trend observation and a picture begins to form. If the pressure is rising, and so is the temperature, a warm front may be just to the south and the low pressure system may be some distance to the west. If the temperature is rising very slowly day-to-day, yet the pressure is falling, a cold front may be to the northwest.

With these two marvelous facts in your hands, it may seem that some sort of an accurate idea of what the weather is going to do is possible. *Wrong again.* Only after you consider the wind direction and velocity can a half-accurate guess be made. Low pressure systems are the troublemakers; therefore, in the next example we must take their circulation into consideration. North of warm fronts, the flow is normally southeasterly. But ahead of cold fronts that have no warm front associated with them, the flow may also be southeasterly. In the latter case, watch the direction for a longer period of time to be sure of the conditions that are approaching. If the warm front is far to the north of your position or nonexistent, the flow may eventually swing to the east. It has been my experience that east winds preceding a cold front mean precipitation. More simply, the low pressure center is south and west of your position, putting you on the northwest corner. In the winter, this situation is most often a blizzard builder.

Back to the warm front: Many times these animals can pass through an area without much adieu. The only clue to their passage is the switch in the wind to the southwest. The pressure may rise or remain nearly the same. It isn't an easy task picking up on these subtle hints that nature leaves.

Wind velocity (or intensity, as I like to think of it) is a great help in predicting. The more intense a system, the quicker the pressure will change as it approaches or you approach it. High wind simply means a cantankerous old son-of-a-gun. Besides witnessing the pressure falling, the intensity of the wind is directly proportional to the pressure gradient of the storm system.

I remember watching a television weatherman up in Northern Michigan where I was fortunate to live for a few years. Every night as he read the latest local conditions he'd make the same comment. He wasn't a degreed meteorologist and so his comments were understandable. It seems that he would always introduce the dewpoint with "Now for all you dewpoint fans out there, it is 39 degrees." Obviously, this individual had no idea of the importance that dewpoint plays. We know it to be related to the amount of humidity in the air, and the humidity is important in forecasting the likelihood of precipitation. If the warm north-flowing air mass is relatively dry, often the front that arrives later is also dry. Remember this point when you see humidity or dewpoint. The closer the dewpoint is to the temperature, the higher the humidity. As I write this, for example, there is a front approaching from the north and expected to be in the area in about 36 hours. The humidity is only running 39%, however. The prospect for a deluge of precipitation at this point when the front arrives is very poor. Humidities in the upper 60s is more consistent with wet weather.

As with flying in general, many factors figure into forecasting the weather. The best flight instructors can help a student learn to land an airplane by breaking the event into its various components and discussing them one at a time. The best pilot predictors of weather, coincidentally, are those who break the weather into its various components and then make a judgment on what they have seen. Applying what we have discussed in this chapter thus far and combining it with our ability to read clouds puts us miles ahead of where we started this book in forecasting (and even "nowcasting") the weather.

The Flight Service Station System

There are two good reasons for reading this book and learning something about weather forecasting. One, the weather changes from minute to minute and being able to note and anticipate those changes will at some time in the future save you the embarrassment of finding the seat of your pants on the upper branches of some tree. Two, the professional weather briefer on the other end of the phone may know very little about the atmosphere and how it changes.

A few facts may be in order to back up this statement. In 1961, The National Weather Service was in charge of hiring and firing all weather briefers. They were also responsible for their schooling. This seems very logical, but the U. S. government has never been very successful with logic; four short years later it turned over the schooling of briefers to the FAA. At this time the FAA took what the weather service had done very well and formalized it and institutionalized the school. Being very smug about this accomplishment and comfortable with their course of instruction, the FAA soon felt that they could hire anyone off the street and make a competent weather briefing specialist out of him or her. The sad fact is that many of the briefers we talk to daily have never been in an airplane and yet are charged with helping pilots out of some special emergency situations. Folks, they are hiring personnel who don't know cumulus from Shinola.

The school for these FSS specialists-to-be is at the FAA Academy in Oklahoma City. At this same institution the FAA teaches air traffic controllers, technicians, and briefers. The FSS classes for the weather briefers are 15 weeks long and begin every four weeks. There are about 22 or 23 students to every FSS class. As intensive as the program is structured to be, you would think that the FSS specialist's specialty would be weather, right? Unfortunately, that is wrong even though it seems perfectly logical. (But we have already talked about the FAA's logic.) Of the 600 hours of classroom instruction, each specialist-to-be receives only 78 hours of weather training. Only 1/6 or less, actually, of the intense training is on weather. This 78 hours only runs about two weeks.

How much weather can these individuals be exposed to in only two weeks?

The weather course is taught by ten fine meteorologists. The students cover such subjects as differential air masses, thunderstorm development, icing, density altitude, highs and lows, and various weather maps. The emphasis is on the main aviation hazards such as low ceilings and visibilities. Although the training is intense, there is very little actual weather-watching incorporated into the course. In all honesty, though, each briefer after leaving the academy goes out into the field and is required to qualify there as capable. In the academy the problem seems to be one of getting the neophyte weather observer to conceptualize how the atmosphere changes and the effects that has on aviation. It is a real problem for most of the students when the only weather they see is at the end of the course—and then that is only what they see after being assigned.

The whole course is graded as you might imagine. How else would the certifying agency know if a weather briefer can make the grade? The bulk of their 600 hours of classroom study is geared in the mechanics of using various equipment as well as the mechanics of giving a briefing. The students, after initial introduction to their jobs, are graded four times near the end of the course. They are graded on how well they volunteer information to a pilot (actually their instructor) as well as how organized the briefing is. It is during this time period that the specialists-to-be learn the phrase "Not recommended for VFR flight." If a student can give these briefings without the interjection of aid from their instructor, he passes. If the briefings are piecemeal and irregular and "the phrase" is not used as much as needed, the student busts out.

As you can see, the background of most FSS personnel is not what most pilots think or even hope it to be. Now in all respect to these people, there are many who mature into fine briefers and eventually get into their jobs. Our problem as pilots is that when we pick up the phone to dial a Flight Service Station, we never know what sort of briefer we will be in touch with. And frankly, the phrase "VFR flight not recommended" is only for the legal protection of the FAA. Just because some 78-hour weather wizard says not to go seems to me to be the worst sort of advice for a pilot who is charged with the final responsibility and conduct of each flight. Believe me, folks, if you know the old "1,000 feet and three miles" rule for VFR flight, you should be able to make up your own mind if the weather is VFR or not. Flying is one of the last bastians of heartfelt freedom and it is disappearing fast. The bottom line is, know what is good for yourself and what you can handle. Be ready to extract a "great" weather briefing from the greenest of FSS specialists—and there are ways of doing just that.

Getting a Great Weather Briefing

Since the Federal Aviation Regulations require us to get a good weather briefing from the FSS or NWS before each flight, we need to know how best to go about it. Lots of times we don't need the whole shootin' match. One afternoon I came to work right after the noon weather presentation on television. I had a clear idea as to the position of all fronts and pressure systems in the United States. It was forecast clear and the satellite photos showed that would probably be true. My evening's flights would be within this clear area.

The phone rang. "Wichita Falls Flight Service."

"Yeah, what are the Dallas area winds aloft please through 12 thousand."

"What's your number?"

"Uh, Metro 1021 I think. What are the Dallas area winds aloft through 12 thousand?"

"Where are you going, Metro?"

"Lawton, Wichita Falls, and Dallas—three round trips tonight. Do you have the winds aloft for the Dallas area through 12,000 feet?"

"Do you have the terminal forecast for DFW?"

"Well, it's going to be clear isn't it? How about the winds aloft?" And so on the story goes. The briefer finally said, "If you'd just let me give the whole briefing I'd cover everything."

But I didn't *need* the whole briefing. While this guy was side-stepping my main question, there were probably several others trying to get a briefing and getting nothing but a busy signal. The point is that in some circumstances and some days, full briefings are not needed—especially if the pilot has acquired information from other sources. On a longer flight from Lawton to DFW to Houston I might need or want a full briefing. On most days I do not, and therefore try to keep the conversation short. This sort of thinking is particularly important since much of the briefing system is now concentrated in major cities by the use of toll-free WATS lines. Calling Oklahoma City Flight Service almost always results in the receiving of a tape recording, stating that all the briefers are busy or drinking coffee or something. The upshot of this is that the fellows at my airline rarely call the number and tend to call either Wichita Falls or company dispatch for the weather.

Let's say you need a full weather briefing. What is the best way to go about it and why should you even bother if you can forecast your own weather? First, there has to be a certain number of basic facts from which you can infer for yourself as to what the weather will do. I do not advocate bypassing the FSS briefings, but suggest that you attempt to supplement that briefing in a most efficient way. Therefore, a good weather briefing makes it a great deal easier to notice changes in the National Weather Service's forecast.

The Synopsis

Every good briefing must cover at least one main point, and that is the "big picture" or synopsis. Without this information, you have not received a good briefing in my opinion. Admittedly, there are times you can skip it when you already know the synopsis from watching television weather, for example.

The synopsis should be considered as the present position of all fronts and pressure systems. Familiar questions when talking over the synopsis with a briefer are: Is that cold front fast-moving? Where is its low pressure center? Are the isobars close together near that low? The answers to these questions will tell you a couple of things. For instance, whether the cold front will move across the intended route of flight in the time period in question. Also, you will learn if turbulence is to be expected due to high winds and if extra fuel is needed to fly against it. In this example, please note that cold fronts can be interchanged with warm fronts.

It is also most important in my opinion to begin the weather briefing with the synopsis. The result is that the remainder of the briefing makes a great deal more sense. When the briefer gets to the Terminal Forecasts, for example, it will be clear to you what is the origination of the weather there.

The FA or Area Forecast

Probably the most neglected piece of information in the hands of the briefer is the Area Forecast. These people just seem unaware that it exists. The synopsis is fine for the overall national picture, but ordinarily we fly in a particular region. The Area Forecast is just that—a regional forecast. Most of the time it predicts things like expected cloud cover and expected precipitation. The most important thing found within the FA is the expected time of frontal passage in an area.

The Area Forecast is very similar to the local picture on the local television weather program. Often, these stations get these FAs as well as the FSS. They tend to concentrate on a geographical region that has similar weather characteristics and terrain. The FA supplies and is the sole source for one important piece of information, the freezing level. In wintertime, this information is golden.

After requesting the synopsis and FA from the briefer, you can let him run. Provided you have already advised him of your intended route and whether or not you can fly IFR, he will provide the rest. In fact, you may have to ask him to slow down as he/she runs helter-skelter through the latest terminal forecasts for major airports along the route of flight. The briefer will punctuate the briefing with the latest hourly sequence reports for the same airports. As an added extra, he may even throw in the winds aloft. Right here is where you may have to stop him and ask for additional information. In the wintertime, the temperatures at the various flight levels is important to supplement the information on the freezing level. Ask these of the briefer so you can discern if, in the event of ice, you should climb the plane or descend.

Airmets and Sigmets

When I hear the word *Sigmet* I can only think of the time that I didn't request "any Airmets or Sigmets" from the briefer. As you probably know, Airmets are warnings that pertain to airmen and aircraft that potentially hazardous conditions exist to those of limited experience or equipment. Sigmets are hazardous to *all* aircraft regardless of size. Well, in Clevelend that day I blundered and didn't ask for the Sigmets. As luck would have it, the briefer did not offer them.

Turbulence is one of the most difficult things to forecast. Often it involves information known only to the weather service because of their technology. I refer to things such as the stability index and K factor. Heck, from watching the TV and receiving a good briefing (at least I *thought* it was at the time), there was no indication of the turbulence to come. Only fair weather cumulus graced the airways and that is all that was predicted. But the turbulence, *oh* the turbulence—I thought for sure that we'd have a 60° dihedral in our wings before we arrived at our destination airport.

The local FSS had all the answers when we got back. I called them within five minutes of taxiing in. Surely, I asked, there must be a Sigmet for turbulence in Michigan? And the casual reply was, "Was it rough?" *Was it rough?* Good grief, that guy had a sadistic sense of humor! The only thing I can say is that *never*, to this day, do I hang up the phone after a briefing until I find out about Sigmets.

We should emphasize that Sigmets and Airmets don't always mean there will be turbulence. Often they are issued for low ceilings and visibilities and icing conditions. You might pick up ice on any cold day if it is cloudy. Some days are just worse than others and the NWS usually earmarks those days for us with a warning of some sort.

Radar Summary

The best weather briefings are polished off with the radar summary. It is easy for you to predict precipitation along a route of flight, especially if you know that there is already some falling. Although the radar summary is often old, it has some use. Basically, it will outline any areas where precip is falling or expected to fall. You are therefore forewarned and will watch for it. If the Flight Service unit that you are talking with has a radar screen on hand, the benefit to you cannot be matched. Knowing where precip is falling is called by the weather service as "nowcasting." In effect, you can do the same "nowcasting" for yourself for your intended route of flight.

As we have seen in this chapter, a great deal of information is available to you. You have the television programs to provide the big picture and day-to-day conditions such as pressure, wind, humidity, etc. With this alone, you can make inferences or forecasts about the weather on your own. I find that I am as accurate as the NWS and often notice changes before they are broadcast over the media. On this point alone could rest the successful outcome of many flights. And, I must admit, there are days when I am wrong and the weather service is right, but I have never been wrong in flight about a weather decision and I will tell you why. For those who observe and really see, all the signs are there. Ominous signs such as clouds and rain of the various types can make their point well. They almost seem to speak, "go back, go back." So if you see—*really* see—you should never have a problem.

Flight Service Stations serve their purpose. For those of us who like to predict the weather conditions ahead as a challenge and a hobby, a good briefing is essential. The briefers do have their handicaps and not all of them are mental. The computer displays instead of the old teletype strips are becoming more commonplace. The result is not a faster dissemination of information, but rather a slower one.

The best pilots take everything into account. Every service

that is available will be used to its fullest extent. Their experience grows more rapidly, and as a result the inflight decisions become easier. That is why they are considered to be the best by their peers.

Chapter 6

Thunderstorms

If you fly, there will come a time that you will have to make a decision about thunderstorms. This chapter looks at the occurrence of these cumulo-giants, explains what creates a storm, what goes on in the guts of one, and what it can do to an aircraft. Later in the chapter we will look at the practical techniques of flying thunderstorms.

Thunderstorms are most numerous in tropical regions. In the mid-latitudes, such as the U.S., the greatest occurrence of storms is in the spring, summer, and fall. Even the Arctic occasionally experiences a storm.

Figures 6-1 through 6-5 show the areas of most frequent occurrence of thunderstorms in the 48 contiguous states. It is interesting to note how many more storms occur in the southeast and south central portions of the country. It is also interesting how the number of storms varies from season to season.

A thunderstorm needs three things to develop. The meanest and ugliest of all storms all have an appetite for the same things. First, there must be a sufficient supply of water vapor. Days of high humidity will fill this bill. Secondly, there must be an unstable lapse rate. This means that as the air rises, it does not cool as readily as it should. Thirdly, there must be a source of lifting. Lifting can come from several sources. Surface heating, converging winds, sloping terrain, frontal systems, or any combination of the above can cause sufficient lifting for thunderstorm generation.

Thunderstorms all begin in the same fashion. There must be an

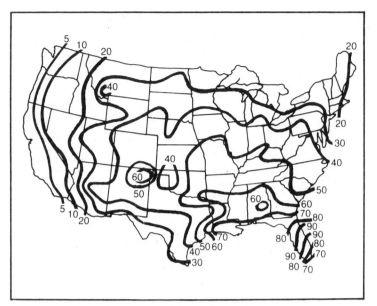

Fig. 6-1. Average number of thunderstorms each year.

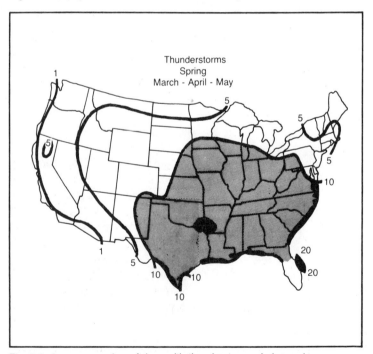

Fig. 6-2. Average number of days with thunderstorms during spring.

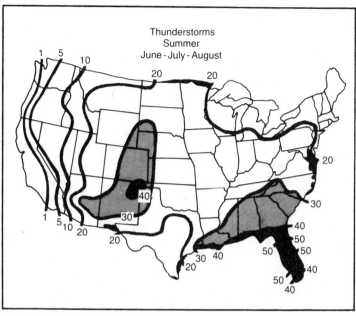

Fig. 6-3. Average number of days with thunderstorms during summer.

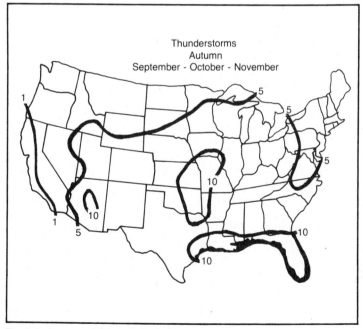

Fig. 6-4. Average number of days with thunderstorms during fall.

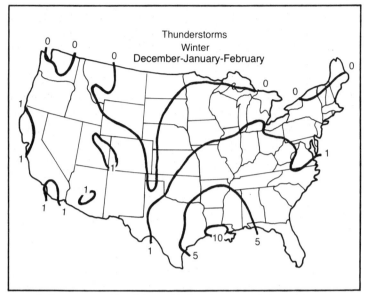

Fig. 6-5. Average number of days with thunderstorms during winter.

initial updraft. The only thing that varies is the cause of the lifting. The updraft moves upward to some point where the water vapor that it is carrying condenses and becomes visible. This condensation causes a release of heat, called the *latent heat of condensation*. This is the effect of adding buoyancy to the air or reinforcing the updraft in a way. The added heat, then, propels the cloud skyward and for a while the entire process is self-sustaining.

Life Cycle of a Thunderstorm

As with frontal waves, thunderstorms have life cycles. Three stages of thunderstorm development are described. First, there is the *cumulus stage*. Second is the *mature stage*. And third is the *dissipation* or *dying stage*. When thunderstorm cells are in clusters or in lines, it is probable that the various storms will be in any one of the stages. The differences between stages are subtle. At no one instant in time can an observer determine the progress from one stage to another, but they all start and end the same way.

It can be said that all thunderstorms are cumulus clouds. It cannot be said, however, that all cumulus clouds become thunderstorms. When in the initial stage of development (or cumulus stage) the cloud is all updraft. The strength of these updrafts are often in the neighborhood of 3,000 feet per minute. Not many airplanes have that sort of climb rate. It is therefore highly improbable that you could outclimb the upward-shooting cloud.

In the infant stages of cumulus development, the water droplets are of extremely small size. As the updraft carries them upward, they become larger and eventually are carried through the freezing level. Flight through this area of the cloud might damage an aircraft. Though it is not known precisely what the freezing level has to do with triggering precipitation, storms do not begin to precipitate until the cloud has grown through this level. As the drops begin to fall, they carry super-cooled air with them, perpetuating the downdraft.

The appearance of rain at the bottom of the cloud heralds the initial part of the mature stage. With the rain falling, the cooler upper air follows it on down. The speed of these downdrafts is in the area of 2,500 feet per minute. All the while there are continuing updrafts of equal magnitude. The vertical wind shear set up at this time may be too much for any airplane to handle. At the bottom of the cloud the downdrafts spread out and cause a surge at the surface, both in wind and pressure. This is called a *plow wind*. Due to the origin of this wind, a sharp temperature drop is usually noticed. The "first gust" is associated with this plow wind and often does the most damage by overturning things on the ground. Needless to say, it is a very bad time to land or take off.

At some point, though, the cloud becomes all downdrafts. With the airmass variety of storms it is interesting that their overhanging clouds cut off sunlight to the ground and negate the lifting force. In a way, they cause their own demise. When there is no more lifting, the water vapor is no longer lifted up to the freezing level. The dissipation stage becomes complete as the rain ceases to fall. All that is left of the once-virile and potent storm is a harmless mass of gray cloud.

All thunderstorms get fairly big. They range in diameter from less than five miles to more than thirty. The bases can be just a hundred feet or so above the ground to more than 10,000 feet. A rule of thumb is that the later in the summer it is, the higher the bases usually are—which is another way of saying that spring storms have lower bases than their summer cousins. The tops of thunderstorms vary greatly. I have been flying around the monsters of Tornado Alley for so long that it is hard to believe that storms can have tops as low as 25,000 feet. Reminiscing, though, I recall the storms in the Great Lakes region were just about that.

One odd event that I was fortunate to witness was a thunderstorm that was only about 9,000 feet tall—a real midget, but it rained bucketsful they say. When you fly freight late at night you get to see all sorts of weather. As we flew into Pittsburgh about midnight in June the ATIS was giving a thunderstorm in progress. Trying to stay above most of the clouds, all of us freighters were staying high until close to the airport. Several of us were talking on the radio to each other (122.9) about the lightning ahead. The odd thing was that it seemed to be coming from below our altitude of 12,000 feet. Pressing on, we reached the tops of the clouds at 9,000 feet. Just prior to our entrance there was one last dying flash. We turned to the left about 25° and popped out of the clouds north of the area that was active. As the old turbine Beech-18 sloshed onto the runway it was apparent there had been a lot of rainfall from somewhere.

Most of the storms that amount to anything are in the neighborhood of 35,000 to 45,000 feet tall. Several times each summer a few giants lurk in the night to harass even the highest-flying aircraft. It is hard to imagine, for example, a Boeing 727 level at 39,000 feet being some 30,000 feet below the top of the storm. Very few storms get this tall and it is easy to see why—70,000 feet is along way from earth. It works out to be about 13 miles.

The severity of storms is normally equal to their duration. Earlier we discussed the life cycle of an air mass thunderstorm. On the average these cells last about an hour. They are producers of moderate wind and precipitation. On the other hand, storms that are found in lines and clusters can last several hours. These are the severe ones. High wind, hail, outlandish turbulence, and flash flooding are their hallmarks. These are the storms known as "steady state."

Steady state storms are usually associated with some sort of weather system. Primarily, cold fronts, squall lines, upper level troughs, and dry lines are the running grounds for the greatest of these merrimakers. Afternoon heating also plays a large part in increasing the intensity of the steady state.

There is one great difference between the air mass and a steady state thunderstorm. That difference is the location of the precipitation with respect to the updrafts. In an air mass-type of thunderstorm, the rain falls next to the updrafts. The friction from the downdrafts created by the rain eventually changes the momentum of the storm to *all* downward, thus destroying the storm from within. With the steady state storm, the rain falls outside the area of the updrafts, hence its innate longevity (Fig. 6-6). The mature stage updrafts are stronger since they are not being weakened and so can persist for several hours.

Thunderstorm Hazards

Most of us are familiar with the various hazards that thunderstorms offer. But did you ever think that all of the possible hazards to an aircraft exist in many thunderstorms? That's right, you can find everything from tremendous turbulence and low ceiling and visibility down to icing. It's all there, rolled into one package. I suppose that the worst possible condition to handle would be to have an inch of clear ice on the wing, hail pounding on the airframe, and 60 mph vertical wind shears whistling in my ears. It's all there if you blunder—the excitement, the helplessness, and the tragedy.

Tornadoes

One of my great ambitions is to fly through a funnel cloud. Of course, there is a stipulation: I want to do it in an Army tank. Since they haven't yet made tanks aerodynamic, my dream will just have

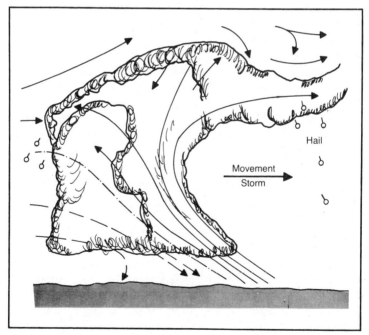

Fig. 6-6. A schematic of a steady state thunderstorm. The updrafts are unimpeded by the precipitation falling outside the updraft area. The steady state storm can be the most violent of storms.

to wait. You probably get the point. Tornadoes may be the greatest hazard to aircraft that there is. What's more, they may be the most insidious.

The strongest storms draw huge amounts of air into their cloud bases to feed their updrafts. If this air has any rotational moment at all, the likely result will be a vortex or tornado. The wind velocity inside a tornado can reach 200 knots and inside the pressure is extremely low. Those tornadoes that do not reach the ground are called "funnel clouds." When one of these funnel clouds makes contact with the ground it becomes known as a tornado. Thunderstorms occur offshore as well and when one springs a funnel cloud to the water it is called a *waterspout*.

I have had the good fortune to see a waterspout close at hand. The experience was something very different. We were stationed about 90 miles offshore on a drilling platform in the Gulf of Mexico. A storm grew up within about five miles of us. Soon it had a small funnel-like appendage protruding from underneath. It was hardly noticeable and at least a thousand feet above the water. As the funnel began to grow in length, the water became disturbed less than a mile from the platform. A vortex of water rose out of the sea and slowly climbed upward. The funnel cloud snaked downward from the dark clouds above. For an instant they joined, dancing a mariner's ballet. Then as quickly as it began, they split in the center. The bottom returned to the churning waters below and the top returned to the violent clouds above. I felt as if I had witnessed something sacred—the touching of the sky and sea.

Looking back at the charts early in this chapter, it is plain to see that the Great Lakes area is not plagued with an undue number of tornadoes. It should be mentioned, though, that waterspouts occur over the lakes as well as the ocean.

Tornadoes are usually associated with steady state storms. Air mass-type storms occasionally breed a funnel cloud or two, but the bulk of the damage is done by the other type. Cold fronts and squall lines bear the greatest possibility for finding these vortices. To penetrate a line of storms and run smack into one of these beauts would ruin your whole day. Structural damage would be inevitable. Also, flying on instruments, it is possible to hit one of these vortices hidden deep in the belly of the storm. There is a new model of thunderstorms proposed in the early 1970s that shows two storms joined by a saddle. Within that saddle is a horizontal or diagonally leaning vortex joining the two cells. Pilots have for years been reporting substantial turbulence in clouds between storm cells.

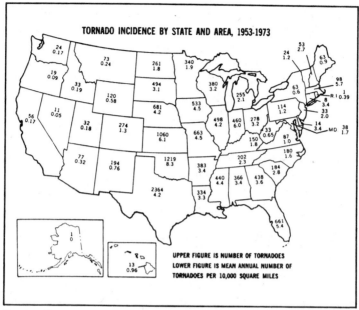

Fig. 6-7. Tornado incidence by state area.

Meteorologists feel that this model is the reason for the turbulence and structural damage done to aircraft passing through this area. Understand that at least one of the adjoining storms has a funnel cloud associated with it.

The funnel-like appendages of thunderstorms are not always directly under a particular cell. A great many of them stretch several miles from the center of the storm. It has also been discovered that funnel clouds are generally generated on the southwest corner of most storms.

A good indicator of a potential funnel outbreak is the cumulonimbus mamma cloud. The mamma cloud is associated with the most violent storms. Their appearance is typified by the mammary-like irregular pockets or festoons protruding below the belly of the storm. Often they are seen hanging from the anvil top close in to the cell. Hourly sequence reports often mention these clouds when they occur. It is a warning of violent weather.

Tornadoes occur most frequently in the Great Plains east of the Rockies. Figure 6-7 shows the state-by-state occurrence of tornadoes from 1953 and 1973. Tornado Alley runs from north central Texas to Kansas, Nebraska, and Iowa. Compare the numbers of funnels through that area with the rest of the United States.

83

Squall Lines

Another of the many hazards of the thunderstorm is the squall line. These lines can be a non-frontal band which may have been generated by a dry line or sometimes just an upper level trough moving through an area. Squall lines, especially in spring and fall, form out front of a cold front—sometimes several hundred miles ahead. These lines form a fashion similar to moving your hand through a bathtub of water. A wave forms out in front of your hand; this would represent the area of lifting causing the squall line while your hand would represent the front. The faster you move your hand, the higher the wave tends to grow. Thus the relationship of squall lines to fast-moving cold fronts. Fast-moving cold fronts are most often the likeliest to spawn squall lines.

The hazard in flying a squall line is the same as an individual storm. The difficulty arises, however, when you want to circumnavigate the problem. A single storm is no problem to fly around. It might not even extend the trip an extra ten minutes. A long squall line, on the other hand, may be too long to go around, and most lines are too severe to think about penetration. The steady state storms incorporated into the line represent just too much hazard to attempt to fly. Their intensity is magnified by late afternoon heating. A good way to plan ahead is to watch either the *Today* or *Good Morning America* weather programs on the day of the trip. Check to see where severe storms are predicted. If they are predicted for your route, leave soon.

Turbulence

Most of what we have been discussing in relation to thunderstorms is turbulence. All thunderstorms contain hazardous turbulence that can damage any plane. The strongest chance of destructive turbulence lies between the vertical updrafts and downdrafts. Turbulence strong enough to break the wings of any plane can be found several thousand feet above the tops of storms. For this reason, turbojets that might top a storm by flying at 40,000 feet must be careful. At high altitudes, jets fly at or near the critical angle of attack. Strong turbulence at high altitude can be enough to upset the balance very easily and a deep stall will occur. So regardless of what most folks think, jets do not always fly over the tops of storms. They go around them. But even this can have its problems. Severe turbulence has been found 20 miles laterally from severe storms.

Low-flying aircraft have big problems too. Most of the general aviation fleet commonly flies below 10,000 feet. When storms are around, you are usually forced to fly quite low. Experience has taught me that 3,000 to 4,000 feet above the surface is the area of minimum turbulence. This has also been supported by atmospheric studies. The real danger of flying low around storms is the plow wind. The plow wind as described earlier is the result of downdrafts spreading out near the surface. The advanced edge of the plow wind is called the "First gust." Often, this area is characterized by the appearance of a "roll cloud." These roll clouds form in the area of first gusts where the plow wind is disturbing smooth air ahead of the storm and causing eddies in the flow (Fig. 6-8). Most roll clouds are very ominous-looking and, for that matter, potentially dangerous. Avoid these *always*. Take it from me, flying through one of these babies is one too many.

Icing

Most of us don't fly in the altitude range where ice is found in thunderstorms. The reason is that the freezing level in summer is normally above 20,000 feet. Nobody, but nobody flies into a thunderstorm at 20,000 feet. To do so invites more than any of us are ready to face. Nonetheless, icing is a hazard. Updrafts support

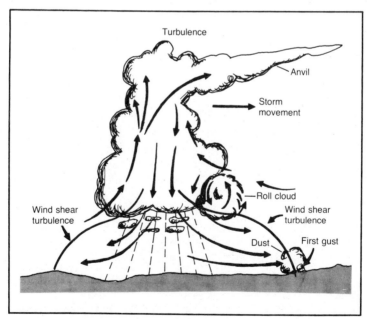

Fig. 6-8. This shows where turbulence may be encountered outside of the cloud.

85

water in its liquid form above the freezing level. The water droplets are supercooled to as much as −15°C. Water in this form may not be ice, yet. Some of it does sublimate into ice crystals.

An aircraft moving through this cooling level disturbs the air. The disturbance causes the droplets to freeze instantly. The result is mixed icing—and if the drops are large enough, rapid clear icing.

Hail

Next to turbulence, the item that will hurt the airplane the most is hail. It is produced in the same way that icing in thunderstorms is produced. The only difference, though, is that the updrafts keep the original frozen droplet suspended above the freezing level. More droplets adhere to the core and the hail becomes larger and larger. The size of hail is directly proportional to the severity of the storm.

Hail is not normally found within a main rain shaft. The hail is ordinarily popped out the top, similar to a hot air popcorn machine. Because of this, hail may fall miles in advance of the main rain shaft. It is distributed from the upper level winds which blow the anvil top to its flat shape, hence the hail fall from the anvil area.

It doesn't take much hail to damage an airplane. Hailstones one half inch in diameter are enough to change the shape of your wing's leading edge.

Low Ceiling and Visibility

Running a close race with a thunderstorm to the nearest airport can sometimes be a poor choice—especially if you lose. As if the plow wind is not enough to fight, low ceilings and visibility may be. Thunderstorm clouds are dense. The visibility in one is near zero. On the ground, the visibility can be zero due to a couple of factors. The rain can be so heavy as to limit any sort of view out the windscreen. The first gust usually stirs up enough dust to create a visibility hazard. When you combine this with all of the turbulence at hand, instrument flight becomes almost impossible.

The low ceilings are most often encountered in the spring. As we discussed earlier, springtime storms generally have lower bases. What is hardest to get under is the roll cloud. These may only be a hundred feet or so off the ground (Fig. 6-9).

Electricity

Lightning in a storm is thought by most of the nonflying public to be deadly to the average airplane. The statistics show however,

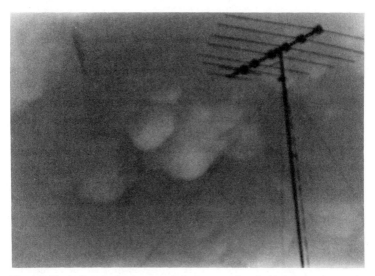

Fig. 6-9. The hallmark of extreme turbulence associated with thunderstorms are these cumulus mammatus clouds.

that lighting is becoming less of a hazard to even groundbound Earthlings. The number of lightning-related deaths has dropped steadily from 1940 to only 67 in 1979. An airplane has little attraction, electrically speaking, to the average lightning bolt. At worst it is just a cockpit annoyance.

Lightning has hit airplanes, though. When it does, its damage is ordinarily slight. Skin punctures are normal and are usually the size of a half-dollar. The important damage, from the standpoint of safety of flight, is that it may knock the Nav and Com radios out. To add insult to injury, your magnetic compass will probably be magnetized and therefore useless.

There are a few horror stories of lightning strikes exploding fuel vapors in the fuel tanks. While this has happened, most recently with a Swissair 747, the odds are extremely high against it happening at all. Jet fuel has been shown to be more readily ignited from lightning than aviation gasoline. To make myself absolutely clear, I actually speak of the fuel *vapors*, not the fuel itself.

The real hazard in flying in close proximity to lightning is blindness. Nearby flashes will blind cockpit crews. If the aircraft is in turbulence at the time, momentary blindness may cause loss of airplane control. Since the days of flying DC-3s, crews have used the technique of lowering their seats as far as possible and turning the instrument lights up to full bright.

Now for a few pointers on lightning:

- ☐ The more frequently a cloud is lighting up, the more severe you can figure it to be.
- ☐ Increasing frequency of lightning displays means the storm is in its mature stage or growing in strength and intensity.
- ☐ Decreasing frequency of lightning flashes means the storm is dying or dissipating.
- ☐ Distant flashes over the horizon along a long sector of horizon surely means a squall line.

Flying Thunderstorms: The Decisions

Thunderstorms are so much a part of the weather that to think about flying without contending with them is to limit yourself extensively. Therefore, a knowledge of thunderstorms is necessary to enjoy flying to the fullest. It may seem suicidal to the average private pilot, but the reality is that some of us fly thunderstorms daily or nightly. The fact that most of us are still here to talk about it must mean that we are doing something right. Everyone's advice is *do not fly through thunderstorms*. But flying through thunderstorms is not what we do as professionals. We fly through areas and lines of thunderstorms where there are gaps. Only a few desperate times have I been in the bowels of one of the monoliths.

Several years ago I made a living flying a Federal Express contract (not to say I was employed by Federal Express). The route was from Minneapolis to Pittsburgh with an intermediate stop each way in Chicago. On a route as long as that one, it's not unusual to fly through a frontal system somewhere. A system that will be burned into my mind forever lay across the route for an entire week, moving slowly. We had to fly it twice each night.

There are a few techniques that you can use to get through a line of T-storms. The structure and intensity of the line dictate the possible options. For example, it is fairly easy to fly around isolated cells of the air mass-type of storm. Fast-moving cold fronts with or without squall lines are a horse of a different color. The difference between the two can be likened to driving a car around through a mostly empty parking lot and driving one against the traffic light at a busy intersection. And when you talk about flying warm fronts, you talk about a game of blind man's bluff.

Flying around air mass storms is the easiest. It can be done almost mechanically. I taught this technique to my private pilot students when I was instructing: Imagine a cell sitting directly over your intended course. All you have to do is to skirt around it, correct? Wrong again! The most important thing is to determine which direction the storm is moving. That direction is pointed out by the anvil head. It points in the direction the storm is moving. The best idea is to go around a storm on the windward side. The storm is moving to the lee.

Once you have established which way the storm is moving, eyeball a heading that will take you around. If you are heading 100° and a 30° deviation will take you around it, fly 055° or 130° depending on storm movement. As you leave your original course, check your time. If it takes you ten minutes to clear the storm, it will take about ten minutes to get back on course. To navigate back to your original course, double the original deviation of 30°. Steer either 055° or 130° and that will bring you back to the original course.

When the cold front or squall line enters the flying picture, the stakes get high. Only professionals should enter this realm. If you are trying to be a professional with little experience, the decision requires a little audacity. There may not be any old bold pilots, but there are just as few meek pilots who still have jobs. My advice to low-experience pilots is to avoid fronts like the plague. It is always best to sit out a front and let it pass. The professional often cannot justify this unless the weather is the absolute worst because he gets paid to find a way around weather.

When you are flying a payload like Federal Express, which absolutely positively has to be there overnight, the times that you can call it quits are few, so you find ways to complete the trip and keep the wings on at the same time. Lines of steady state storms can be penetrated if they are broken. The big problem is deciding where the best place to punch through actually lies. Many times, though, there are large gaps where everyone is going through. Such was the case in July of 1977. One of the longest lines of storms that I have seen in my career stretched from Traverse City, Michigan to Dubuque, Iowa. In that distance there was only one hole, through which tons of aircraft metal poured. The storms were building along the front and everyone held the same playing cards, large and small aircraft alike.

Deciding where to go through the wall in this case was easy. For the 30-minute period prior to arriving at the hole, we had heard all the others ahead of us reporting good rides from 8,000 feet up. Stealing along at 9,000 feet, we had every right to expect a good ride. We were not disappointed. Shooting through a hole at least 30 miles wide, we remained VFR most of the time. The view that evening was spectacular as we watched our high-altitude brothers sliding between the sparking towers of cumulus on either side.

Flying thunderstorms is best when in the IFR environment—or when you have a clearance, I should say. Paradoxically, though, the object of getting a good ride is maintaining VFR. Flying without airborne radar almost requires that you stay out in the open. What about ATC's radar? Well, it *is* better than nothing, but its usefulness to you more often than not hinges on the controller behind it.

The digitalized radar used today does a great deal to make weather less visible and the aircraft targets more visible. When storms are heavy, the precip shows up fairly well, but not 100%. Remember, radar paints precipitation but not turbulence and clouds. Ordinarily, turbulence is found where precip shows up, but it can be lots of other places as well. All of this is for naught if the controller working you doesn't give a hoot if your wings get rocked or not. Some of these guys just tell you to deviate as you want and then you are on your own. I'd like to grab some of these guys and jack their chairs up and down to remind them that it is not as smooth above as it is down there in that control room.

Let's look at the things that we really have to do when we get right up against it. The number one item is to remain VFR if at all possible. This applies to *everyone* in *any* equipment at *any* altitude. The chances for survival when you stay VFR is near 100% all of the time. Once you get yourself into the clouds, things become very sticky and chancy. Lines of thunderstorms just do not descend upon you like falling rocks; you always have some amount of time to look them over as you drive up to them. It is best to query the controller as to how long and how thick the disturbance is. Ask if there are any holes and if so, what sort of ride others are getting. There are going to be a few times though when you will be the first one through. Pioneering a line of steady state storms can be a memorable experience.

Once a hole has been decided upon, it is time to choose the altitude at which you would like to be. If there is prior information from others going through, request that altitude or the nearest one you can get. If clouds will be penetrated, use 3,000 to 4,000 feet above the ground. Of course, if staying higher will keep you out of the clouds, by all means stay higher! Request these altitudes as early as possible. The Eastern states have more traffic, and as a result it may take a great deal longer than you had hoped for before they work you into the requested altitude. Try your best to be level and not in a descent as the area in question is entered. It is no time to have extra airspeed.

As we mentioned earlier, flying in close proximity to storms at night may cause a blindness problem. Turn the lights on the panel to full bright. If you have the choice between red and white light, use white. Adjust the seat as low as possible. The idea is to expose yourself to as little of the flashing as you can. Tighten the seat belt and wait for something to happen. At this point, leave yourself an out or at least know how much you can take before quitting. Don't be numb to the fact that it might just be too much to handle. If it's too scary, do a 180° turn. The turn should be completed before entering a cell. Trying to execute a turn in an angry cloud has been the end of a few good pilots. Once inside a cell, the shortest way out is straight ahead. You can expect lots of hot-tempered updrafts and downdrafts. Don't worry about altitude; just keep the wings level and stay close to that heading. If you are worried about IFR separation, don't be. The controller already knows you are the only idiot in there. As quickly as the whole thing started, it will end.

Punching a line of storms is usually the shortest and quickest way to the destination. On occasion, the lines are too solid or thick and penetration becomes too awesome a job. One front in August that we flew grew to very thick proportions between Cleveland and Rosewood, Ohio. Strolling up to the front, we queried the controller. He said it was about 40 miles thick, and about 60 miles thick the direction we were going. At 4 o'clock in the morning, no one else was going through. My Captain, stern of jaw, said he was going to try it. Tremendous lightning filled the air. We started in and immediately started out. Glad to be out of the teeth of that monster, we landed and checked with Flight Service. Go south, they said, around the end, and so we did—no rain, no turbulence, a good ride.

The following week took the prize for the damnedest thing I have ever seen. Another so-called line was waiting for our return trip into Chicago. The tops were reported to 48,000 feet—strong storms for this part of the country. As luck would have it, Center was sitting on their lip. The controller supplied us with no information whatsoever. That left us looking out the window, since we had no on-board radar. The lightning was flashing from every direction. We slid between the first two cells at 6,000 feet because it was between layers. Inside the treacherous area, it was like walking through a mine field. The task was just to dodge the next brilliant flashing cloud. Zipping out the back and about 40 miles from where we entered, the mercury-vapor-lighted horizon of Chicago appeared. The ride? Perfect—not a bump, we didn't even get wet!

In the western part of our country there are rocks in the thunderstorms. At least that is how it seems. Flying around storms out west is an exercise in avoiding storms while avoiding mountains. The air is a little more dry and the result is higher bases. Sometimes this makes VFR possible. At night, however, forget VFR and file IFR. The MEAs out west will ordinarily put a pilot around 10,000 to 14,000 feet. This means that most of the time in thundery weather the plane might be flying in cloud. Without airborne radar you must simply rely on the controllers. It's a better deal out west, though, because the controllers' workload is less and they have more time to help out.

Airborne radar is the nicest thing going for flying in thundery weather. I wouldn't exactly say it eliminates all chances for developing ulcers, but it does minimize the problem. We won't fully discuss radar here, but a few words are in order. Radar falls into the category of "nowcasting." You can pick out the large holes from quite a way out. Courses can be adjusted much earlier and most trips finished a little quicker. Often it saves the day.

Every front is a little different. The techniques remain the same. The prudent pilot knows his limitations and will stop before he gets in over his head. To learn to fly heavy weather will take time, a touch of boldness, and a little luck. Remember, the best method is to stay VFR. The experience will come a little slower that way, but that is the way we want to do it.

Chapter 7
Winter's Challenge

Every season of the year has a personality. Winter has *two*. The howling fury of a late afternoon blizzard is soon forgotten in the silvery morning light that follows as it glints off a snow-draped kingdom. The clear days of winter are punctuated with the churning of light aircraft engines glad to be about. But on the gloomy days, the air is conspicuously deserted as owners and airplanes stay huddled inside.

A great deal more utility could be wrung from each airplane if the hazards of winter could be foreseen and understood. In this chapter we will look at those hazards and what brings them about. Possibly, after reading this, the changes will be easier to anticipate. Then you can utilize the flying techniques outlined in the later portion of the chapter.

What are the hazards of winter flying? For one thing, you get the lowest ceilings and visibilities of the year. Fog is often a deterrent to even the IFR pilot because there are times that the visibility is simply too low. Snow is another factor. Although it is beautiful, it's no fun to clear the wings before flight. And snow showers enroute must often be avoided due to the lowering visibility. Blowing snow is as bad as a foggy day and ice on the runways causes control problems. IFR flight takes on the added risk of airframe icing and anybody can expect induction icing.

There they are, the culprits of winter—seven things that must be considered every time you fly. The hope is that you learn to deal with them in a positive manner. Every year a full 25% of fatal aircraft accidents can be attributed to pilots who continued VFR into adverse weather conditions. We want to avoid that and that is why you are here.

The Ballad of Miller Farr

The weather was snowy
It was blowing a gale;
The ice on the wipers
Was telling the tale.
The visibility was a mile; maybe two,
But Miller was convinced
He would make it on through.

The weather worsened—less than a mile.
His look turned to terror
Now gone was his smile.
Friends, I'm not joking
And this ain't no laugh.
They chiseled this in stone
As his epitaph:

"Here lies Miller Farr
He continued VFR."

Minimum values of ceiling and visibility determine Visual Flight Rules. If the ceiling and/or visibility happens to be below those minimums, then instrument flight is required. Ceiling is the maximum height from which you can maintain visual contact with the ground. You might think of it as having the back of the airplane up against the cloud above. Visibility, logically, is how far you can see. There are two types of visibility. That which characterizes surface weather reports is lateral visibility. It can be measured by knowing visible objects and how far they are. It can also be measured by electronic measuring devices. Inflight visibility is a little different. We find inflight visibility reports with Pireps or reports made by pilots as they move along. This visibility is usually judged on a diagonal from the pilot's perch aloft.

Fog

Fog is a surface-based sort of cloud. It can be composed of minute water droplets or ice crystals. It is the most frequent cause of visibilities below three miles. The rapidity with which fog forms makes it especially hazardous. It can drop from good VFR to below IFR in a few minutes. Several times during the winter months my crew and I have left Dallas/Fort Worth airport for our home base, Lawton, with good visibility reported ahead. When we received our weather for the approach it was almost a shock. We have seen it as low as 100 feet ceiling and one-quarter mile visibility—too low to land. Fog is primarily a hazard during takeoff and landing. It is extremely important, however, for the pilot who is attempting to maintain VFR to be able to see the ground as well.

A small temperature-dewpoint spread is the essential ingredient for fog to form. Coastal areas are plagued by fog regularly due to the abundant moisture. Nevertheless, fog can form anywhere there is abundant condensation nuclei. This is a major reason that industrial areas have high occurrences of fog even if they are inland. The products of combustion supply adequate condensation nuclei to the atmosphere.

There are two processes that cause fog to form. One we have already discussed. When the temperature approaches the dewpoint, fog is likely. If moisture is added to the air near the ground, you may have ground fog.

Radiation Fog

Fog is classified by the forms. *Radiation fog* is shallow, although it may be dense—dense enough to obscure the sky or just part of the sky. Radiation fog's common name is *ground fog*. As viewed from the sky, it may completely cover the ground below you. If flying VFR, it may become impossible to navigate by use of landmarks. But due to its shallow nature, buildings can often be seen popping up through it. Fog during the winter months can be a real problem for both the IFR and the VFR pilot. When snow covers the ground, landmarks are extremely difficult to see. For the IFR pilot, the environment of the runway may appear very hazy indeed, even with the lights.

One of the most surreal sights I have ever seen occurred on a foggy morning in Minnesota. The entire countryside was awash in a sea of milky white fog. As we approached the city it was apparent that an instrument approach was in the offing. It was as if we were at sea, for on the horizon appeared a lighthouse. The tallest building in Minneapolis sat poised among the slow-motion waves of the fog. Bright strobe lights drew the attention of all the airborne mariners in the area—truly a unique and beautiful sight. Also, this one landmark gave us a fixed reference point so that we could keep track of our position and double-check the controller.

Back to the thrust of this book, though: In order to have some idea about when fog will form, you need to know the most likely conditions. Radiation fog thrives on clear nights with little or no wind. These sort of nights, in the wintertime, often follow cold frontal passage by about two or three days. Fog is most likely after the brisk winds die down. If there is adequate moisture, the temperature and dewpoint will be close together. Within the range of 4° Farenheit between the two, fog formation is likely. If the fog does not form by late in the evening around midnight, the next most likely time will be near daybreak. Temperatures tend to plummet a little just before the sun rises. When this occurs, it may be enough to cool the air to the dewpoint and cause fog.

Radiation fog does not occur over water only on land. The reason is that when the ground cools at night, it cools the surrounding air. Water surfaces cool very little from nighttime radiation. The thickness of the fog depends upon the wind conditions. The banks are usually shallow with 5-knot winds or less. With a little higher wind the fog is whipped up, so to speak, and it thickens. Too much wind, about 10 knots, does more to disperse the fog than anything else. On occasion this mixing leads to the formation of a stratus layer on top of the fog.

How long will the fog last? Most radiation fog burns off before noon at the latest. What tends to make fog hang around is the formation of a cloud deck on top of it as we just discussed.

Advection Fog

Another brand of fog is *advection fog*. This kind can be a real problem in the winter for deep continental areas. It doesn't have to be winter for it to form along coastal areas or at sea. Advection fog is formed when moist air moves over colder ground or water. Simply put, the air is cooled to its dewpoint by rubbing up against something colder (Fig. 7-1).

Winds up to 15 knots have the effect of thickening the entire bank. Anything more than about 15 knots tends to turn the fog into low-lying stratus. This can improve the visibility on the ground, but the stratus deck may not rise high enough to allow for successful instrument approaches. The West Coast of the country is particularly vulnerable to this type of fog. It is likely to form offshore in the winter where the water temperature is lower than the land. Then, after it has formed, the fog will steal ashore (Fig. 7-2).

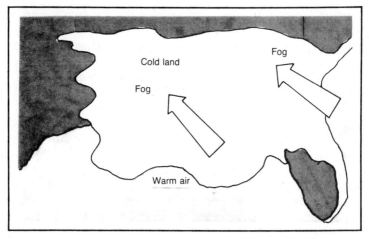

Fig. 7-1. Advection fog over the southeastern U.S. The fog may spread as far north as the Great Lakes.

It gets just tough for the central and eastern areas of the country. Warm Gulf of Mexico air moves in over the colder continent. The result is a widespread fog that often reaches as far north as the Great Lakes. This sort of fog is common in Michigan as the moisture and fog come from the lakes.

From the air you will notice little difference between advection fog and radiation fog. One clue is that advection fog will at times

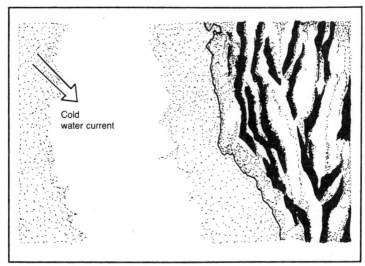

Fig. 7-2. Sea fog, also called advection fog, will form at sea then move inland.

have clouds above. In other words, advection fog can form under cloudy skies. Because of this and the amount of radiation from the sun is cut down, advection fog may be more persistent than the radiation type. It may move in at any time of day or night. Also note that this type of fog is usually associated with warm fronts.

Upslope Fog

Upslope fog requires rapidly rising terrain for its formation. That automatically rules out its occurrence in a great portion of the country. The Appalachians, and predominantly the eastern slopes of the Rockies, experience this phenomenon.

The condition is caused by moist stable air being cooled adiabatically as it is pushed up the terrain. *Adiabatically*, simply means that the normal scheme of things calls for the air to get cooler as altitude increases. Thus, air being pushed upslope cools down. Whenever the wind ceases, the lifting ceases and so does the cooling. The result is that the fog will not form anymore.

Upslope fog can become quite dense. In winter, the possibility exists for icing conditions. Mountain ridges are obscured and VFR is impossible. Upslope fog can be the cause for some great beauty in the mountains. The fog in the winter will actually freeze on the trees. When sunlight finally touches below the thick blanket of cloud, the trees glisten a snowy white. It's almost as if the branches are threaded through popcorn. If it does this to trees that are standing, imagine how it could load up an airframe moving through the mess.

Precipitation-Induced Fog

This sort of fog can form with the advent of rain or snow. It depends on the surrounding air being cooler than the precip. If it occurs during snow conditions, the snow is usually of a wet nature. It is more likely to occur, however, when warm rain or drizzle falls into cool air. It is very similar to the steam you get in the shower. The rain saturates the cool air and visibility rapidly deteriorates. It can be quite dense and cloudlike and very persistent in staying around.

Generally associated with warm fronts, precip fog can be found in association with slow-moving cold fronts or stationary fronts. It tends to be the most hazardous to flight of all the fog types. The reason for this is that along with the precipitation comes icing, turbulence, and storms in the warmer part of the year.

Ice Fog

A true wintertime condition is ice fog. You won't find this one in Texas, dewpoint fans. The temperature needs to be well below the freezing mark. About 25 degrees below zero is a good starting place. The moisture sublimates out of the air into tiny ice crystals. Ice fog is known more for its occurrence in the Arctic region, but finds its way into the U.S. snow belt every year.

The one hazard other than slight structural icing is vision. Pilots have reported being blinded while flying through this phenomenon towards the sun.

Precipitation

The most common cause of low visibility is precipitation. Rain, drizzle and snow all limit visibility to varying degrees. Drizzle and snow limit visibility to a greater degree because of their finer texture or particle size. Drizzle often occurs in stable air, and fog is likely to be its running mate. But snow is probably the greatest limiter. Visibility can be zero in heavy snow.

Rain seldom causes visibility to fall below one mile. The exception of course is heavy rain. Cockpit visibility is another matter. With snow sticking to the windscreen or rain streaming across it, the visibility might only be from your nose to the window.

Icing

Icing can occur during any time of the year. In the more temperate climates, such as the United States, we encounter icing more often in the winter. The freezing level is nearer the ground in winter than summer and this allows less room to maneuver below it. More extensive cloudiness from the more frequent cyclonic storms also increases the risk of encountering icing conditions. Polar regions have the heaviest icing conditions in spring and fall. This is because much of the winter the temperatures are too cold to retain much moisture, which is necessary for icing conditions.

Fundamentally, there are two types of icing: *structural* and *induction*. The former affects the ability of the wing to do its job. The latter limits the engine in doing its job of providing thrust.

Two conditions are necessary for the formation of ice on the airframe in flight. First, you must be flying through visible moisture. This can be clouds or rain or snow. Secondly, the temperature of the airframe must be 0°C or colder. It is possible for an airframe to be cooled to a temperature below ambient air temperature due to the airflow around the surfaces. It is also possible in aircraft moving faster than 180 knots indicated to have an airframe temperature a few degrees higher than ambient temperature due to frictional heating.

Supercooled water droplets is a term we should define. When a substance is supercooled, its temperature is below 0° C but it hasn't frozen yet. This can be attributed to the droplet being agitated enough to resist stabilization. Supercooled water increases the accretion rate significantly. Since supercooled water is in an unstable liquid state, the way in which it freezes is a little extraordinary. When the aircraft strikes an area of supercooled water droplets, part of the drop freezes on contact. The latent heat of fusion released by this freezing melts the remaining portion of the drop. The rest of it may freeze as it moves rearward from the slipstream. The form that this latter part takes determines the type of icing. There are three types of structural icing: *clear, rime,* and *mixed.* Each has its identifying features (Fig. 7-3).

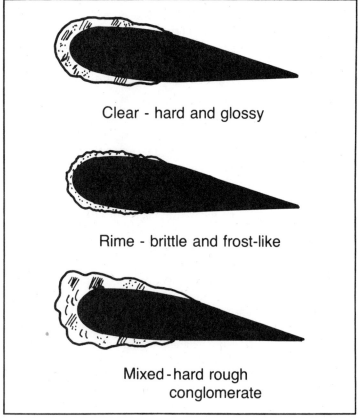

Clear - hard and glossy

Rime - brittle and frost-like

Mixed - hard rough conglomerate

Fig. 7-3. Three kinds of icing on airfoils.

Clear Ice

Clear ice is formed when the remaining portion of a droplet does not freeze on impact. Instead, it flows with the slipstream back along the contour of the surface. It makes a smooth sheet of clear or transparent ice. Clear icing forms when the droplets are large. Rain and cumuliform clouds are the most likely source.

Figure 7-3 shows the difference between ice types. The clear ice is very hard, heavy, and sticks like bubble gum to the bottom of your shoe. Removal by deicing equipment is fairly difficult.

Rime Ice

Rime ice is formed by small water droplets. Stratiform clouds or light drizzle produce this kind of icing. The droplets freeze rapidly upon impact and do not spread out along the surface. It gets its white sucrosic-type of texture by trapping air as it freezes, and hence its lighter weight. Its irregular shape and rough texture are the reasons why it is such a good spoiler of lift. Besides its different appearance, another way to identify it is by the way it builds outward from aircraft surfaces.

Mixed Ice

The term *mixed icing* should leave no doubt in your mind. It is a mixture of the two types of ice we have just discussed. It forms when the droplets vary in size. It can form just as rapidly as the others, sometimes faster. Occasionally it builds out into the slipstream in funny mushroom shapes—if icing can be considered funny.

One thing should be mentioned and made clear about how icing affects an airplane. The old-timers will tell you that the airplane cannot hold up the additional weight. As a result, the pilot must start a descent or stall out. In fact, that is not true at all. The weight of ice on an airplane can be measured in ounces with the exception of large transports. What actually happens is that the airfoil of the wing is altered to a shape that is not as aerodynamically efficient as the one the engineers designed. Also, the interrupted airflow causes the airfoil to seek a higher angle of attack to produce a given amount of lift. Eventually the critical angle-of-attack will be exceeded and the wing will stall. Recovery from a stall with a less-than-efficient wing draped with ice can be "iffy." *If* it recovers, you have been lucky. If it doesn't, you won't do it again.

Icing and Cloud Types

Wherever there is a cloud below freezing temperature there exists the potential for structural icing of the airframe. Drop size, distribution, and aerodynamic forces all play a part in the type of ice that will form. In certain instances, where icing potential exists, ice will not form.

The most favorable condition for the formation of ice is where there are a large number of large drops. This tends to cause a high rate of accretion and clear icing. Conversely, when only a relatively few drops of small size exist in a cloud, the rate goes down accordingly.

Small water droplets are most often associated with fog or drizzle. When these conditions occur there is normally no appreciable amount of precipitation. The result is rime icing.

Normally, we think of stratus clouds as the producers of rime ice. When stratus clouds become thick and stratified, the opposite can occur. Altostratus and nimbostratus can be the cause of continuous rain. The upshot of this is a high number of large water droplets, the formula for clear ice. These stratified clouds in winter can cover extensive areas—thousands of square miles. The effects can be extremely dangerous for protracted flights.

The amount of water that can remain suspended in a cloud is related to the temperature. Warm air can support more moisture. Using this hypothesis, then, you can expect the greatest amount and rate of icing to occur in the first few degrees below freezing. In actual flight research, continuous icing conditions have seldom been found more than 5,000 feet above the freezing level. What we are saying here is that the temperature usually decreases with altitude, and therefore there is less moisture for ice to form at those altitudes.

The lifting force associated with the formation of cumulus clouds gives favorable support to large droplets and high numbers of the same. Whenever an airplane enters a heavy water concentration, the drops break and slide rapidly back the aircraft surface. The water as it moves aft forms a solid sheet of clear ice. Pilots usually avoid cumulus clouds for obvious reasons.

The upper limit of icing potential in cumuliform clouds cannot be specified. The cellular nature of their form, however, is thought to reduce the amount of continuous icing that can exist in a horizontal direction. The only time it might prove to be more hazardous than the norm is for flights through broad zones of showers.

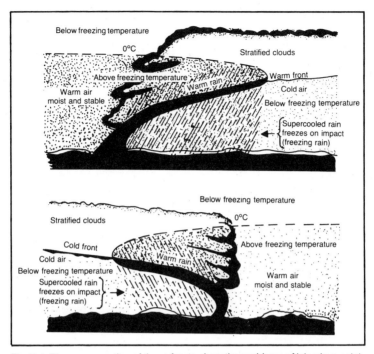

Fig. 7-4. The cross-section of these fronts show the problems of icing in precipitation. The warm front is on top and the cold front is on the bottom.

Fronts and Icing

Fronts play an important part in winter flying. Because of the readily available moisture and cold temperatures, icing can be a critical factor. The condition most often encountered that produces the most ice is from warm air aloft. The warm air (above freezing) is lifted by the frontal slope. At some point it begins to fall, and it falls into the below-freezing temperatures below. The droplets become supercooled and are just waiting for something to latch onto. Along comes Peter Pilot in his shiny new Wombat 250 and picks up a load of ice. It doesn't matter if it is a warm front or a cold front as Fig. 7-4 shows. The result is the same—a pack of ice.

Terrain

Terrain can be an important consideration for avoiding ice. As we discussed earlier in this chapter, air moving upslope cools adiabatically. It becomes visible and at below freezing temperatures is ready to make ice. Flying near mountainous terrain increases the risk for icing. Mountain ranges cause this rapid upward movement of air on the windward side. Essentially, what we have then are vertical currents. As we have said several times before, lifting causes the larger type of droplet. Combine this with a front moving across the mountains and it gets crazy.

Every mountain range affects icing conditions in its own special way. Mainly, the wind flow up the ridges controls where ice will be found. Of course, it will be on the windward side, but the ridges that are perpendicular to wind flow will have the greatest hazard. The highest icing potential lies above the crest and on the windward side. From the bottom of the cloud up to about 5,000 feet above the mountain top is the icing zone. If the clouds are cumuliform, the zone may extend much higher.

Flying in the Ice

It probably is not forecasting in the truest sense of the word, but when you are already aloft you need to make decisions, though, about whether to continue or divert in some manner. Being able to interpret the weather pattern as it stands when considering an inflight action is weathercasting. So that is what we will talk about in this section.

In flying ice, there are no cut-and-dried rules. The old-timers always say to climb. They may be right. How else did they get old? The problem is that a climb may not always be possible in a light aircraft for many reasons. If there is a secret to flying ice successfully, it is in getting a good preflight briefing, being able to notice weather changes, and plenty of experience at both. No one is born with experience, so it may be possible to get in a little deep sometimes. Flying ice, however, is usually not as dangerous as it is nerve-wracking.

When getting a preflight briefing on icy days, the most important information comes from the winds aloft forecast and knowing the predicted freezing level. The item to watch for is a temperature inversion (Fig. 7-5). Normally, the atmosphere gets colder with altitude. This fact is important to the pilot again and again. An inversion is an area in the vertical direction where the normal temperature trend does not get colder. Rather, it gets warmer or stays the same for several thousand feet. Temperature inversions can be found anywhere in the atmosphere at any time of the year. In winter, however, they are usually between 4,000 feet and 9,000 feet with the exception of the tropopause.

The temperature inversion can be a great advantage in making a flight in winter. If the temperature is above freezing above the inversion's base, that altitude will be free of ice. Even when flying a de-ice and anti-ice equipped airplane, it is the best policy to fly at ice-free altitudes.

Recognizing the type of ice that is forming on the wings can be of utmost importance. We discussed rime ice earlier. From that discussion you should know that rime ice is associated with stratiform clouds. With all the other information in this book on stratus clouds, you know that the layers will not be very thick. You can know this in 99% of the cases if you are not encountering any precipitation. And remember, rime ice does not form during precipitation, except for drizzle.

Once you have established that you are flying in stratiform clouds, you must make a decision. The first decision should be to get out of your present altitude. Let's give you some more information: You are cruising at 6,000 feet. On the climb up to 6,000 you remember being between layers at 5,000 feet. The winds aloft forecast, on the other hand, spots an inversion somewhere above 6,000 feet. Do you climb or do you descend where you might be between layers and free of ice?

Either way you go *might* be correct. You don't know where the tops are, but 7,000 feet should be above freezing. Since free air between layers often pinches out or truncates, that between-layers condition might not be below you anymore. The best choice in this

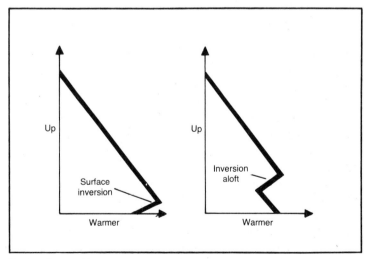

Fig. 7-5. Inverted lapse rates or "inversions". A lapse rate is a decrease temperature with altitude. Shown here are a surface inversion and an inversion aloft.

case is to climb. Most wintertime flying (except near fronts) reveals that the tops of the stratus layers are in the same range as the inversions—4,000 to 9,000 feet. The chances are that you will top the entire mess at 7,000 feet in this instance. If not, you will probably still be above freezing. And if that is not the case, you can always request 5,000 feet and go looking for that between-layers condition you noticed on the way up. Also, if the free air between layers is not there anymore you have already started a descent. All you have to do is continue your descent to an alternate airport and get out of the ice or get below all the clouds altogether.

Flying through clear icing conditions requires a quicker and more deliberate action. Clear icing, as we have mentioned, comes from cumuliform clouds and the rate of accretion is high. The highest rate of icing usually takes place in upper portions of the cloud. If you are flying near the top, you usually know it. The sunlight comes blistering through in an unbearable white glare. In most cases, a short climb of a thousand feet or so will get you into the sun.

If the clear ice accretion is due to precipitation, the situation can get desperate in a flash. The rain and sleet slapping against the windscreen are warning enough to do something. If you do anything but descend to the nearest coffee shop, you are asking for a beating of the worst kind.

So there it is, flying ice in a nutshell. De-icing equipment is nice, but it has the reputation of only delaying the inevitable. Don't wait. Do one of three things when flying ice: Get up, get down, or get out.

Winter flying can be the best flying of the year. On clear days the air is so *very* clear. The rides are often smooth above the clouds and you have the privilege of seeing the sun when earthbounders do not. Summer weather changes faster than winter and takes a different sort of moxie. Winter weather changes are more insidious because they are so often hidden by clouds. It takes a *real* weather watcher to be any good at it. Invest the effort. It will pay handsome dividends.

Appendix
Accident Statistics with
Weather as a Causal Factor

Earlier in this book we laughed about good ol' Miller Farr and how he continued VFR. But Miller was only one of many pilots who get in over their heads every year by not reading the signs of the weather. The National Transportation Safety Board has been kind enough to supply us with some safety information and statistics that will be presented here. Following are two recent Safety Information bulletins dated August, 1981.

NTSB Finds Too Many Inadequate Weather Briefings to GA Pilots

General aviation pilots too often do not receive all the weather information they should have when they are briefed before by Flight Service Station personnel before or during flight, the NTSB reports.

The Safety Board investigated 940 general aviation accidents in 1980. A special Board investigation showed that in six of the 72 weather accidents analyzed by Board meteorologists in 1980—more than eight percent—weather briefings by FSS personnel were inadequate. The Board termed this "alarming."

The Board found that the Federal Aviation Administration's FSS weather briefers had been adequately trained, and the weather information that the pilots should have been given was available before the briefings were given. In all six cases, however, FSS personnel did not follow FAA procedures for giving all pertinent information in weather briefings for pilots.

In five of the cases, briefers did not give pilots all pertinent enroute or destination weather, including warnings of thunder-storms, icing, turbulence, or weather that called for instrument flying. The Board cited "inadequate/incorrect weather briefing" as a factor in reporting on all five accidents.

In the sixth accident, the pilot changed his destination after being briefed, but the Board said there was "serious deficiency" in the briefing that he had been given for his original destination.

The Safety Board found that FAA's review of audio recordings of weather briefings is the best way to monitor the adequacy of weather information that pilots receive, but that only 40 percent of current Flight Service Stations have recording equipment.

The Board recommended that FAA permanently audio-record all weather briefings by FSS personnel, and monitor recordings to see that all FSS personnel follow FAA weather briefing procedures.

Board Urges Non-Instrument Rated Pilots to Develop a "Turn Back" Psychology in the Face of Weather

The National Transportation Safety Board said the safety record of general aviation could show dramatic improvement if non-instrument rated pilots faced with adverse weather conditions could learn the life-saving value of two words: Turn Back.

Despite decades of repeated warnings, the phrase "continued VFR flight into adverse weather conditions" continues to appear with disheartening regularity as a probable cause of accidents.

In releasing Issue No. 7 of 1980 civil aviation "Briefs of Accidents," the Board cited 8 accidents in which "continued VFR flight into adverse weather conditions" was the cause of the accident.

A typical profile of this type of accident as it appears in Brief No. 7 involved a non-instrument rated pilot of a Mooney M-20C who was killed when he crashed near Elk, California. The pilot, who had not filed a flight plan and was not known to have obtained a weather briefing, encountered fog near Elk with a ceiling of less than 100 feet. But he elected to continue the flight and was seen by witnesses at treetop level prior to the crash.

Decisions to "turn back" may cause pilots and passengers inconvenience but the Board's accident statistics plainly show that for many non-instrument rated pilots, the alternative can be a fatal accident.

Pilots who consider themselves "professionals" should guide themselves by these rules when coping with possible weather problems along a proposed line of flight:

1. Get a weather briefing. Adequate briefings, properly un-

derstood and applied, are the best basis for determining whether your flight should be executed as planned.

2. Establish clearly in your mind the current enroute conditions, the enroute forecast, and the "escape route" to good weather.

3. Once you begin your flight, update your weather information frequently.

4. Unless you are instrument-proficient and have an instrument-equipped aircraft, avoid areas of low ceilings and visibilities.

5. File an appropriate flight plan.

After looking through all the relevant statistics, one fact is glaringly apparent: The airlines have the lowest accident statistics. The commuters are next best and general aviation lags far behind. There are two main reasons for the differences. Certificated air carriers have the most stringent training guidelines and the experience level of the average pilot in command is in the thousands of hours. The commuters are starting to catch up to this standard of excellence since the advent of the "hard core" guidelines set forth by the FAA in 1978 under FAR Part 135. As a matter of fact, accidents for the commuters dropped significantly in 1978 after the rules began to be enforced.

General Aviation, on the other hand, has been touched very little by rule changes since 1976. And those changes seem to do very little for the overall picture of General Aviation. You might notice a decline of total accidents after 1979. I feel that this is a direct result of higher avgas prices that in turn keep pleasure flying to a minimum. Basically, over the past 10 years the accident rate for general aviation has remained about the same while the air carriers have been improving, and 1980 was a banner year yielding no accidents for the major carriers.

Typical Weather-Related Accident Reports

In the following pages we will look at quite a few general aviation accidents that were caused at least in part by the weather conditions at the time. One thing I would like to point out: In most instances, an accident is not caused by *one* main factor, but rather by *several* factors piling up on the pilot until the culmination of an accident. The way to play the game is to stack the cards in your favor and keep an ace in the hole.

I picked these reports at random with the exception that I attempted to find one or two in every region of the United States. There seem to be more accidents with pilots flying with VFR flight plans or no flight plans than those flying on IFR flight plans. Those accidents that occurred while flying on an IFR flight usually exceeded the aircraft's ability to fly in that type of weather.

The point is that you should know your limitations and your aircraft's limitations. Also, the overall optimism of pilots is amazing. One main fact should be stressed here, if it wasn't stressed in the book. If the weather is so low that you have to get very low to dodge it, you should turn around. The reason for this is simple: Areas of low ceilings are generally widespread and part of a complex system. It often takes hours and sometimes days for the system to move out of an area. For you to think that the weather will improve in only a few more miles or a few more minutes is usually baseless.

Another important fact comes to the surface from the random choice of these reports. There are a few which note that the pilot's blood alcohol level was high. We all know what that does to decision-making. So why drink and then fly? If you want to drink and fly, take airlines.

One more important item is the lack of good weather briefings. The Safety Notice at the front of this section has already expounded on this. The safe outcome of flights though, depends on these things.

1. Know your own limitations and the limitations of the aircraft you are flying.

2. Get a good weather briefing.

3. Don't be an optimist. Rather, be a realist and know the point at which you will venture no further.

4. Don't mix alcohol and flying unless it is for windshield de-icing.

Explanatory Notes

U.S. general aviation refers to the operations of U.S. civil aircraft owned and operated by persons, businesses, corporations, etc., excluding the operations of U.S. air carriers.

U.S. air carrier operations include the following three operational categories: certificated route air carriers; supplemental air carriers; and commercial operators of large aircraft.

The following definitions contained in CFR 49, Part 830, paragraph 830.2, apply when used in this publication.

Aircraft accident: An occurrence associated with the operation of an aircraft which takes place between the time any person boards the aircraft with the intention of flight until such time as all such persons have disembarked, and in which any person suffers death or serious injury as a result of being in or upon the aircraft or by direct contact with the aircraft or anything attached thereto, or in which the aircraft receives substantial damage.

Fatal injury: An injury which results in death within seven days of the accident.

Serious injury: Any injury which (1) requires hospitalization for more than 48 hours, commencing within seven days from the date the injury was received; (2) results in a fracture of any bone (except simple fractures of fingers, toes, or nose); (3) involves lacerations which cause severe hemorrhages, nerve, muscle, or tendon damage; (4) involves injury to any internal organ; or (5) involves second- or third-degree burns, or any burns affecting more than five percent of the body surface.

Substantial damage: (1) Except as provided in subparagraph (2) of this paragraph, substantial damage means damage or structural failure which adversely affects the structural strength, performance, or flight characteristics of the aircraft, and which would normally require major repair or replacement of the affected component. (2) Engine failure, damage limited to an engine, bent fairings or cowling, dented skin, small punctured holes in the skin or fabric, ground damage to rotor or propeller blades, damage to landing gear, wheels, tires, flaps, engine accessories, brakes, or wingtips are not considered "substantial damage" for the purpose of this part.

Injury index: Refers to the highest degree of personal injury sustained as a result of the accident.

Type of accident: Relates to the immediate circumstances of the occurrence. Many accidents involve a series of circumstances and therefore require a second type to more fully describe the sequence of events. Some examples of types of accidents are as follows:

- ☐ *Gear collapsed:* Collapse of the landing gear due to mechanical failure other than malfunction of the retracting mechanism.
- ☐ *Gear retracted:* Retraction of the landing gear due to malfunction or failure of the retracting mechanism or to inadvertent retraction by the crew. Excludes intentional gear retraction and wheels-up landing.

☐ *Airframe failure:* Occurrences resulting from failure of any part of the airframe while in flight or in motion on the ground. Excludes failure resulting from contact with another airplane or object, or impact with the ground, or damage from landing gear collapse or retraction.

☐ *Engine failure/malfunction:* Occurrences of engine failure or malfunction for any reason. Includes engine stoppage, power interruption, or power loss, actual or simulated.

Phase of operation: Relates to the particular segment of the flight or operation during which the circumstances of the accident occur.

Kind of flying: Refers to the purpose for which the aircraft is being operated at the time of the accident. There are four broad categories of kind of flying, as follows:

☐ *Instructional Flying:* Refers to flying accomplished in supervised training under the direction of an accredited instructor.

☐ *Noncommercial Flying:* Refers to the use of an aircraft for purposes of pleasure, personal transportation, or in connection with a private business in corporate/executive operations, and in other operations, wherein there is no direct monetary fee charged. It includes the following categories:

Pleasure: Flying by individuals in their own or rented aircraft for pleasure, or personal transportation not in furtherance of their occupation or company business.

Business: The use of aircraft by pilots (not receiving direct salary or compensation for piloting) in connection with their occupation or in the furtherance of a private business.

Corporate/executive operations: The use of aircraft owned or leased and operated by a corporation or business firm for the transportation of personnel or cargo in furtherance of the corporation's or firm's business, and which are flown by professional pilots receiving a direct salary or compensation for piloting.

☐ *Commercial flying:* Includes all general aviation flying normally conducted for directed financial return, except instructional flying. It includes air taxi operations, aerial application, fire control, aerial mapping or photography, aerial advertising, power/pipeline patrol, and fish spotting.

☐ *Miscellaneous flying:* Includes other kinds of flying not covered under the other three broad categories. In some instances the criterion of direct financial return may or may not be present.

Collision between aircraft: Collisions between aircraft are so classified only when both aircraft are occupied. This includes collisions wherein both aircraft are airborne (midair); one is airborne, the other on the ground; and both are on the ground. A collision with a parked, unoccupied aircraft is classified under the broad category of collision with objects (parked, unoccupied aircraft).

Causes and related factors: In determining probable cause(s) of an accident, all facts, conditions, and circumstances are considered. The object is to ascertain those cause/effect relationships in the accident sequence about which something can be done to prevent recurrence of the type of accident under consideration. Accordingly, for statistical purposes where two or more causes exist in an accident, each is recorded and no attempt is made to establish a primary case. Therefore, in the Cause and Related Factor Table, the figures shown in the columns dealing with cause will exceed the total number of accidents. The term *factor* is used, in general, to denote those elements of an accident which further explain or supplement the probable cause(s). This provision was incorporated in the coding system to increase its flexibility and to provide a means for collecting essential items of information which could not be categorized elsewhere in the system.

Aircraft weight categories: The International Civil Aviation Organization's categories of aircraft weight are utilized to classify accident data as follows:

0—2,250 kilograms	(0—4,960 pounds)
2,251—5,700 kilograms	(4,961—12,565 pounds)
5,701—27,000 kilograms	(12,566—59,525 pounds)
27,001—272,000 kilograms	(59,526—599,650 pounds)
272,001 kilograms and greater	(599,651 pounds and greater)

Small fixed-wing aircraft: Fixed-wing aircraft which have a maximum gross takeoff weight of 5700 kilograms (12,565 pounds), or less.

Large fixed-wing aircraft: Fixed-wing aircraft which have a maximum takeoff weight greater than 5,700 kilograms (12,565 pounds).

Rotorcraft: Aircraft which in all usual flight attitudes are supported in the air wholly or in part by a rotor or rotors; i.e., by airfoils rotating or revolving about an axis.

Types of weather conditions: The types of weather conditions (VFR/IFR) are determined in accordance with the prescribed minima in Part 91 of the Federal Aviation Regulators. These minima pertain to the ceiling and visibility, in conjunction with the type of airspace, at the accident site. Type of weather conditions are based on surface weather as determined from officially recognized sources. Weather conditions encountered in flight are not necessarily representative of the classifications VFR/IFR as carried under Type of Weather Conditions.

FILE	DATE	LOCATION	AIRCRAFT DATA	INJURIES F S M/N	FLIGHT PURPOSE	PILOT DATA
3-2116	2/27/78 MERRILL PASS, AK TIME - 1325		EVANGEL 4500 N4508L DAMAGE-DESTROYED	CR- 1 0 0 PX- 2 0 0	COMMERCIAL AIR TAXI-PASSG	AIRLINE TRANSPORT, AGE 35, 5500 TOTAL HOURS, 1203 IN TYPE, INSTRUMENT RATED.

DEPARTURE POINT
  DILLINGHAM, AK
TYPE OF ACCIDENT
  COLLISION WITH GROUND/WATER

INTENDED DESTINATION
  ANCHORAGE, AK

LAST ENROUTE STOP
  STONY RIVER, AK
PHASE OF OPERATION
  IN FLIGHT UNCONTROLLED DESCENT

UNCONTROLLED

PROBABLE CAUSE(S)
  PILOT IN COMMAND - INADEQUATE PREFLIGHT PREPARATION AND/OR PLANNING
  PILOT IN COMMAND - CONTINUED VFR FLIGHT INTO ADVERSE WEATHER CONDITIONS
  PILOT IN COMMAND - SPATIAL DISORIENTATION
FACTOR(S)
  WEATHER - LOW CEILING
  WEATHER - RAIN
WEATHER BRIEFING - SELF-HELP, PILOT CHECKED WEATHER DATA
MISSING AIRCRAFT - LATER RECOVERED

SKY CONDITION
  OVERCAST
VISIBILITY AT ACCIDENT SITE
  ZERO
OBSTRUCTIONS TO VISION AT ACCIDENT SITE
  UNKNOWN/NOT REPORTED
TYPE OF FLIGHT PLAN
  VFR
FIRE AFTER IMPACT
REMARKS- WX CONDITION IN PASS RPRTD BY PIREP.RECOVERY DATE 2/28/78.

CEILING AT ACCIDENT SITE
  0
PRECIPITATION AT ACCIDENT SITE
  RAIN
TYPE OF WEATHER CONDITIONS
  IFR

FILE	DATE	LOCATION	AIRCRAFT DATA	INJURIES F S M/N	FLIGHT PURPOSE	PILOT DATA
3-1049	3/7/78 NR.TRADING BAY,AK TIME - 1630		PIPER PA-20 N7151 DAMAGE-DESTROYED	CR- 1 0 0 PX- 0 0 0	NONCOMMERCIAL PLEASURE/PERSONAL TRANSP	COMMERCIAL, AGE 49, 518 TOTAL HOURS, 277 IN TYPE, INSTRUMENT RATED.

DEPARTURE POINT
SNIPE LAKE,AK

INTENDED DESTINATION
LAKE HOOD,AK

TYPE OF ACCIDENT
COLLISION WITH GROUND/WATER   CONTROLLED

PHASE OF OPERATION
IN FLIGHT NORMAL CRUISE

PROBABLE CAUSE(S)
PILOT IN COMMAND - CONTINUED VFR FLIGHT INTO ADVERSE WEATHER CONDITIONS
PILOT IN COMMAND - MISJUDGED ALTITUDE
FACTOR(S)
WEATHER - LOW CEILING
WEATHER - FOG
WEATHER - SNOW
WEATHER BRIEFING - NO RECORD OF BRIEFING RECEIVED
WEATHER FORECAST - FORECAST SUBSTANTIALLY CORRECT

SKY CONDITION
OBSCURATION

CEILING AT ACCIDENT SITE
UNKNOWN/NOT REPORTED

VISIBILITY AT ACCIDENT SITE
1 MILE OR LESS

PRECIPITATION AT ACCIDENT SITE
SNOW

OBSTRUCTIONS TO VISION AT ACCIDENT SITE
FOG

TEMPERATURE-F
27

WIND VELOCITY-KNOTS
CALM

TYPE OF WEATHER CONDITIONS
VFR

TYPE OF FLIGHT PLAN
NONE

FILE	DATE	LOCATION	AIRCRAFT DATA	INJURIES F S M/N	FLIGHT PURPOSE	PILOT DATA

3-4361 3/10/78 ANCHORAGE,AK
TIME - 0946

BELLANCA 7GCBC
N57452
DAMAGE-SUBSTANTIAL

CR- 1 0 0
PX- 0 1 0

NONCOMMERCIAL
PLEASURE/PERSONAL TRANSP

AIRLINE TRANSPORT, AGE
31, 6800 TOTAL HOURS,
UNK/NR IN TYPE, INSTRU-
MENT RATED.

NAME OF AIRPORT - ANCHORAGE INTL
DEPARTURE POINT   INTENDED DESTINATION
CAMPBELL LAKE,AK   TALKEETNA,AK
TYPE OF ACCIDENT
TURBULENCE
COLLISION WITH GROUND/WATER   UNCONTROLLED

PHASE OF OPERATION
IN FLIGHT NORMAL CRUISE
IN FLIGHT UNCONTROLLED DESCENT

PROBABLE CAUSE(S)
PILOT IN COMMAND - IMPROPER IN-FLIGHT DECISIONS OR PLANNING
MISCELLANEOUS - VORTEX TURBULENCE
FACTOR(S)
PILOT IN COMMAND - FAILED TO FOLLOW APPROVED PROCEDURES,DIRECTIVES,ETC.
WEATHER - LOW CEILING
WEATHER BRIEFING - NO RECORD OF BRIEFING RECEIVED

SKY CONDITION   CEILING AT ACCIDENT SITE
OVERCAST   800
VISIBILITY AT ACCIDENT SITE   PRECIPITATION AT ACCIDENT SITE
5 OR OVER(UNLIMITED)   NONE
OBSTRUCTIONS TO VISION AT ACCIDENT SITE   TEMPERATURE-F
FOG   34
WIND DIRECTION-DEGREES   WIND VELOCITY-KNOTS
30   4
TYPE OF WEATHER CONDITIONS   TYPE OF FLIGHT PLAN
VFR   NONE
REMARKS- PILOT FAILED TO MAKE RADIO CONTACT IN CONTROL ZONE.ENCOUNTERED TURB 1 1/2MILES SW RWY 6R.

FILE	DATE	LOCATION	AIRCRAFT DATA	INJURIES F S M/N	FLIGHT PURPOSE	PILOT DATA
3-1474	1/16/78 NR.KERNVILLE,CA TIME - 0910		PIPER PA-32 N3350W DAMAGE-DESTROYED INTENDED DESTINATION FRESNO,CA	CR- 0 1 0 PX- 1 0 0	NONCOMMERCIAL PLEASURE/PERSONAL TRANSP	PRIVATE, AGE 43, 965 TOTAL HOURS, ALL IN TYPE, NOT INSTRUMENT RATED.

DEPARTURE POINT
 INYOKERN,CA
TYPE OF ACCIDENT
 COLLIDED WITH TREES

PHASE OF OPERATION
 IN FLIGHT NORMAL CRUISE

PROBABLE CAUSE(S)
 PILOT IN COMMAND - CONTINUED VFR FLIGHT INTO ADVERSE WEATHER CONDITIONS
 MISCELLANEOUS ACTS,CONDITIONS - AIRFRAME ICE
FACTOR(S)
 WEATHER - LOW CEILING
 WEATHER - ICING CONDITIONS-INCLUDES SLEET,FREEZING RAIN,ETC.
 WEATHER BRIEFING - BRIEFED BY FLIGHT SERVICE PERSONNEL, BY PHONE
 WEATHER FORECAST - FORECAST SUBSTANTIALLY CORRECT
 MISSING AIRCRAFT - LATER RECOVERED

SKY CONDITION
 OVERCAST
VISIBILITY AT ACCIDENT SITE
 1/4 MILE OR LESS
OBSTRUCTIONS TO VISION AT ACCIDENT SITE
 NONE
WIND VELOCITY-KNOTS
 34
TYPE OF FLIGHT PLAN
 VFR
REMARKS- RECOVERY DATE 1/18/78.

CEILING AT ACCIDENT SITE
 200
PRECIPITATION AT ACCIDENT SITE
 RAIN, SNOW
WIND DIRECTION-DEGREES
 229
TYPE OF WEATHER CONDITIONS
 IFR

FILE	DATE	LOCATION	AIRCRAFT DATA	INJURIES F S M/N	FLIGHT PURPOSE	PILOT DATA
3-0676	3/2/78 TIME - 2026	DURANGO,CO	BEECH 95-C55 N885M DAMAGE-DESTROYED	CR- 1 0 0 PX- 3 0 0	NONCOMMERCIAL PLEASURE/PERSONAL TRANSP	PRIVATE, AGE 48, 1207 TOTAL HOURS, 275 IN TYPE. INSTRUMENT RATED.

NAME OF AIRPORT - DURANGO LAPLATA
DEPARTURE POINT   INTENDED DESTINATION
  ARLINGTON,TX   DURANGO,CO
TYPE OF ACCIDENT   PHASE OF OPERATION
  COLLISION WITH GROUND/WATER CONTROLLED   LANDING OTHER

PROBABLE CAUSE(S)
  PILOT IN COMMAND - INADEQUATE PREFLIGHT PREPARATION AND/OR PLANNING
  PILOT IN COMMAND - IMPROPER IFR OPERATION
FACTOR(S)
  WEATHER - SNOW
  WEATHER BRIEFING - BRIEFED BY FLIGHT SERVICE PERSONNEL, BY PHONE
  WEATHER FORECAST - FORECAST SUBSTANTIALLY CORRECT
  MISSING AIRCRAFT - LATER RECOVERED

                                          CEILING AT ACCIDENT SITE
SKY CONDITION   1500
  OVERCAST   PRECIPITATION AT ACCIDENT SITE
VISIBILITY AT ACCIDENT SITE   SNOW
  5 OR OVER(UNLIMITED)   TEMPERATURE-F
OBSTRUCTIONS TO VISION AT ACCIDENT SITE   37
  NONE   TYPE OF FLIGHT PLAN
TYPE OF WEATHER CONDITIONS   IFR
  IFR
REMARKS- CIRCLED VICINITY A/P APPROX 4MIN.PLT ACTIVATED RWY LIGHTS NOT ON.RECOVERY DATE 3/3/78.

119

FILE	DATE	LOCATION	— AIRCRAFT DATA	INJURIES F S M/N	FLIGHT PURPOSE	PILOT DATA
3-2262	6/11/78 NR.SILVERTON,CO TIME - 1430		PIPER PA-28 N9669J DAMAGE-DESTROYED	CR- 1 0 0 PX- 3 0 0	NONCOMMERCIAL PLEASURE/PERSONAL TRANSP	PRIVATE, AGE 34, UNK/NR TOTAL HOURS, UNK/NR IN TYPE, NOT INSTRUMENT RATED.

DEPARTURE POINT
  DURANGO,CO
TYPE OF ACCIDENT
  COLLIDED WITH TREES

INTENDED DESTINATION
  GRAND JUNCTION,CO

PHASE OF OPERATION
  IN FLIGHT NORMAL CRUISE

PROBABLE CAUSE(S)
  PILOT IN COMMAND - INADEQUATE PREFLIGHT PREPARATION AND/OR PLANNING
  PILOT IN COMMAND - MISJUDGED DISTANCE,SPEED,AND ALTITUDE
  PILOT IN COMMAND - IMPROPER IN-FLIGHT DECISIONS OR PLANNING
FACTOR(S)
  WEATHER - HIGH DENSITY ALTITUDE

SKY CONDITION
  SCATTERED
VISIBILITY AT ACCIDENT SITE
  5 OR OVER(UNLIMITED)
OBSTRUCTIONS TO VISION AT ACCIDENT SITE
  NONE
TYPE OF WEATHER CONDITIONS
  VFR
FIRE AFTER IMPACT

CEILING AT ACCIDENT SITE
  UNLIMITED
PRECIPITATION AT ACCIDENT SITE
  NONE
TEMPERATURE-F
  72
TYPE OF FLIGHT PLAN
  NONE

REMARKS- ACCIDENT SITE 11000FT MSL.DENS ALT COMPUTED TO BE 14000FT.

FILE	DATE	LOCATION	AIRCRAFT DATA	INJURIES F S M/N	FLIGHT PURPOSE	PILOT DATA
3-3970	12/4/78 TIME - 1945	NR.STEAMBOAT SPGS,CO	DEHAVILLAND DHC-6 N25RM DAMAGE-DESTROYED	CR- 1 1 0 PX- 1 13 6	COMMERCIAL COMMUTER AIR CARRIER AIR TAXI-PASSG. S-D	AIRLINE TRANSPORT, AGE 29, 7340 TOTAL HOURS, 3904 IN TYPE, INSTRUMENT RATED.

DEPARTURE POINT
STEAMBOAT SPGS,CO
TYPE OF ACCIDENT
COLLISION WITH GROUND/WATER   CONTROLLED

INTENDED DESTINATION
DENVER,CO

PHASE OF OPERATION
IN FLIGHT NORMAL CRUISE

PROBABLE CAUSE(S)
WEATHER - ICING CONDITIONS-INCLUDES SLEET,FREEZING RAIN,ETC.
WEATHER - DOWNDRAFT,UPDRAFTS
FACTOR(S)
PILOT IN COMMAND - INITIATED FLIGHT IN ADVERSE WEATHER CONDITIONS
WEATHER BRIEFING - BRIEFED BY FLIGHT SERVICE PERSONNEL, BY PHONE
WEATHER FORECAST - WEATHER SLIGHTLY WORSE THAN FORECAST
MISSING AIRCRAFT - LATER RECOVERED

SKY CONDITION
OVERCAST
VISIBILITY AT ACCIDENT SITE
5 OR OVER(UNLIMITED)
OBSTRUCTIONS TO VISION AT ACCIDENT SITE
BLOWING SNOW
WIND DIRECTION-DEGREES
270
TYPE OF FLIGHT PLAN
IFR

CEILING AT ACCIDENT SITE
UNKNOWN/NOT REPORTED
PRECIPITATION AT ACCIDENT SITE
SNOW
TEMPERATURE-F
26
TYPE OF WEATHER CONDITIONS
IFR

REMARKS- WX EXCEEDED ACFT CAPABILITY TO MAINTAIN FLT.HIT MTN 10530FT MSL.RECOVERY DATE 12/5/78.

FILE	DATE	LOCATION	AIRCRAFT DATA	INJURIES F S M/N	FLIGHT PURPOSE	PILOT DATA
3-1446	6/1/78 TIME - 2200	NR.HERNANDO BEACH,FL	PIPER PA-28R N2291M DAMAGE-DESTROYED	CR- 1 0 0 PX- 1 0 0	NONCOMMERCIAL BUSINESS	STUDENT, AGE 31, UNK/NR TOTAL HOURS, UNK/NR IN TYPE, NOT INSTRUMENT RATED.

DEPARTURE POINT
SARASOTA,FL

INTENDED DESTINATION
PANAMA CITY,FL

TYPE OF ACCIDENT
COLLISION WITH GROUND/WATER   UNCONTROLLED

PHASE OF OPERATION
IN FLIGHT UNCONTROLLED DESCENT

PROBABLE CAUSE(S)
PILOT IN COMMAND - INADEQUATE PREFLIGHT PREPARATION AND/OR PLANNING
PILOT IN COMMAND - CONTINUED VFR FLIGHT INTO ADVERSE WEATHER CONDITIONS
PILOT IN COMMAND - SPATIAL DISORIENTATION
FACTOR(S)
WEATHER - THUNDERSTORM ACTIVITY
WEATHER BRIEFING - BRIEFED BY FLIGHT SERVICE PERSONNEL, BY PHONE
WEATHER FORECAST - FORECAST SUBSTANTIALLY CORRECT

SKY CONDITION
OVERCAST
VISIBILITY AT ACCIDENT SITE
UNKNOWN/NOT REPORTED
OBSTRUCTIONS TO VISION AT ACCIDENT SITE
UNKNOWN/NOT REPORTED
TYPE OF FLIGHT PLAN
NONE

CEILING AT ACCIDENT SITE
UNKNOWN/NOT REPORTED
PRECIPITATION AT ACCIDENT SITE
THUNDERSTORM
TYPE OF WEATHER CONDITIONS
IFR

FILE	DATE	LOCATION	AIRCRAFT DATA	INJURIES			FLIGHT PURPOSE	PILOT DATA
				F	S	M/N		

3-0964	3/2/78 NR.WACO,GA	PIPER PA-30				NONCOMMERCIAL	COMMERCIAL, AGE 36, 371
	TIME - 1945	N7428Y		CR- 1	0	0	CORP/EXEC	TOTAL HOURS, UNK/NR IN
		DAMAGE-DESTROYED		PX- 1	0	0		TYPE, INSTRUMENT RATED.

NAME OF AIRPORT - WEST GEORGIA
DEPARTURE POINT   INTENDED DESTINATION
  CARROLLTON,GA   ALABASTER,AL
TYPE OF ACCIDENT
  COLLISION WITH GROUND/WATER CONTROLLED

PHASE OF OPERATION
  IN FLIGHT CLIMB TO CRUISE

PROBABLE CAUSE(S)
  PILOT IN COMMAND - INITIATED FLIGHT IN ADVERSE WEATHER CONDITIONS
  PILOT IN COMMAND - ATTEMPTED OPERATION W/KNOWN DEFICIENCIES IN EQUIPMENT
  MISCELLANEOUS ACTS,CONDITIONS - AIRFRAME ICE
FACTOR(S)
  WEATHER - LOW CEILING
  WEATHER - ICING CONDITIONS-INCLUDES SLEET,FREEZING RAIN,ETC.
  WEATHER BRIEFING - BRIEFED BY FLIGHT SERVICE PERSONNEL, BY PHONE
  WEATHER FORECAST - FORECAST SUBSTANTIALLY CORRECT

SKY CONDITION   CEILING AT ACCIDENT SITE
  OVERCAST   800
VISIBILITY AT ACCIDENT SITE   PRECIPITATION AT ACCIDENT SITE
  3 MILES OR LESS   DRIZZLE
OBSTRUCTIONS TO VISION AT ACCIDENT SITE TEMPERATURE-F
  FOG   33
WIND DIRECTION-DEGREES   WIND VELOCITY-KNOTS
  90   15
TYPE OF WEATHER CONDITIONS   TYPE OF FLIGHT PLAN
  IFR   IFR
REMARKS- ACFT NOT EQUIPPED WITH ANTI-ICING OR DE-ICING SYSTEMS.

FILE	DATE	LOCATION	AIRCRAFT DATA	INJURIES F S M/N	FLIGHT PURPOSE	PILOT DATA
3-1905	4/26/78 NR.KENNESAW,GA TIME - 1533		BEECH N35 N9495Y DAMAGE-DESTROYED	CR- 1 0 0 PX- 1 0 0	NONCOMMERCIAL PLEASURE/PERSONAL TRANSP	COMMERCIAL, AGE 56, 700 TOTAL HOURS, 133 IN TYPE, INSTRUMENT RATED.

DEPARTURE POINT
NAPLES,FL
TYPE OF ACCIDENT
AIRFRAME FAILURE   IN FLIGHT

INTENDED DESTINATION
CARROLLTON,GA

PHASE OF OPERATION
IN FLIGHT UNCONTROLLED DESCENT

PROBABLE CAUSE(S)
PILOT IN COMMAND - SPATIAL DISORIENTATION
PILOT IN COMMAND - EXCEEDED DESIGNED STRESS LIMITS OF AIRCRAFT
FACTOR(S)
PILOT IN COMMAND - ATTEMPTED OPERATION BEYOND EXPERIENCE/ABILITY LEVEL
MISCELLANEOUS ACTS,CONDITIONS - SEPARATION IN FLIGHT
WEATHER - ICING CONDITIONS-INCLUDES SLEET,FREEZING RAIN,ETC.

SKY CONDITION
BROKEN/LOWER SCATTERED
VISIBILITY AT ACCIDENT SITE
5 OR OVER(UNLIMITED)
OBSTRUCTIONS TO VISION AT ACCIDENT SITE
NONE
WIND VELOCITY-KNOTS
15
TYPE OF FLIGHT PLAN
IFR

CEILING AT ACCIDENT SITE
10000
PRECIPITATION AT ACCIDENT SITE
RAIN
WIND DIRECTION-DEGREES
320
TYPE OF WEATHER CONDITIONS
IFR

REMARKS- NO LOGGED ACT INST TIME SINCE 1974..AIRMET FOR ICING IN CLOUDS.

FILE	DATE	LOCATION	AIRCRAFT DATA	INJURIES F S M/N	FLIGHT PURPOSE	PILOT DATA
3-3199	9/10/78	ALEXANDRIA,LA	BEECH V35	CR- 1 0 0	NONCOMMERCIAL	PRIVATE, AGE 41, 675
	TIME - 1431		N5642S	PX- 0 0 0	PLEASURE/PERSONAL TRANSP	TOTAL HOURS, 491 IN TYPE,
			DAMAGE-DESTROYED			INSTRUMENT RATED.

DEPARTURE POINT   INTENDED DESTINATION   LAST ENROUTE STOP
  MANNING,SC   HOUSTON,TX   HATTIESBURG,MS
TYPE OF ACCIDENT   PHASE OF OPERATION
  STALL, SPIN   IN FLIGHT NORMAL CRUISE

PROBABLE CAUSE(S)
  PILOT IN COMMAND - CONTINUED FLIGHT INTO KNOWN AREAS OF SEVERE TURBULENCE
  PILOT IN COMMAND - SPATIAL DISORIENTATION
FACTOR(S)
  PILOT IN COMMAND - PHYSICAL IMPAIRMENT
  MISCELLANEOUS ACTS,CONDITIONS - ALCOHOLIC IMPAIRMENT OF EFFICIENCY AND JUDGMENT
  WEATHER - TURBULENCE, ASSOCIATED W/CLOUDS AND/OR THUNDERSTORMS
  WEATHER - THUNDERSTORM ACTIVITY
  WEATHER BRIEFING - BRIEFED BY FLIGHT SERVICE PERSONNEL, BY RADIO
  WEATHER FORECAST - FORECAST SUBSTANTIALLY CORRECT

SKY CONDITION   CEILING AT ACCIDENT SITE
  OVERCAST   UNKNOWN/NOT REPORTED
VISIBILITY AT ACCIDENT SITE   PRECIPITATION AT ACCIDENT SITE
  UNKNOWN/NOT REPORTED   THUNDERSTORM
OBSTRUCTIONS TO VISION AT ACCIDENT SITE   TEMPERATURE-F
  BLOWING SAND   83
WIND DIRECTION-DEGREES   WIND VELOCITY-KNOTS
  150   7
TYPE OF WEATHER CONDITIONS   TYPE OF FLIGHT PLAN
  IFR   IFR
REMARKS- BLOOD ALCOHOL LEVEL 70MG PERCENT.

FILE	DATE	LOCATION	AIRCRAFT DATA	INJURIES F S M/N	FLIGHT PURPOSE	PILOT DATA
3-4325	9/10/78 TIME - 1240	NR-MACKINAW CITY,MI	CESSNA 172K NR4380 DAMAGE-DESTROYED	CR- 2 0 0 PX- 1 0 0	NONCOMMERCIAL PLEASURE/PERSONAL TRANSP	PRIVATE, AGE 31, 225 TOTAL HOURS, UNK/NR IN TYPE, NOT INSTRUMENT RATED.

DEPARTURE POINT
  GRAYLING,MI
TYPE OF ACCIDENT
  COLLIDED WITH OBJECT

INTENDED DESTINATION
  MACKINAC ISLAND,MI

PHASE OF OPERATION
  IN FLIGHT NORMAL CRUISE

PROBABLE CAUSE(S)
  PILOT IN COMMAND - CONTINUED VFR FLIGHT INTO ADVERSE WEATHER CONDITIONS
FACTOR(S)
  PILOT IN COMMAND - INADEQUATE PREFLIGHT PREPARATION AND/OR PLANNING,
  WEATHER - FOG
  MISCELLANEOUS ACTS,CONDITIONS - AIRCRAFT CAME TO REST IN WATER
  WEATHER BRIEFING - NO RECORD OF BRIEFING RECEIVED
  WEATHER FORECAST - FORECAST SUBSTANTIALLY CORRECT

SKY CONDITION
  OVERCAST
VISIBILITY AT ACCIDENT SITE
  ZERO
OBSTRUCTIONS TO VISION AT ACCIDENT SITE
  FOG,
TYPE OF FLIGHT PLAN
  NONE

CEILING AT ACCIDENT SITE
  200
PRECIPITATION AT ACCIDENT SITE
  DRIZZLE
TYPE OF WEATHER CONDITIONS
  IFR

REMARKS- BRIDGE.NO WX REQUESTED OR PROVIDED FOR IN BRIEFING FOR MACKINAC STRAITS AREA.

FILE	DATE	LOCATION	AIRCRAFT DATA	INJURIES F S M/N	FLIGHT PURPOSE	PILOT DATA
3-4169	11/22/78 EUREKA,MO TIME - 2030		CESSNA 182C N84R5T DAMAGE-DESTROYED	CR- 1 0 0 PX- 3 0 0	NONCOMMERCIAL PLEASURE/PERSONAL TRANSP	NO CERTIFICATE, AGE 49, 350 TOTAL HOURS, 300 IN TYPE, NOT INSTRUMENT RATED.

DEPARTURE POINT
FENTON,MO

INTENDED DESTINATION
SENECA,OK

TYPE OF ACCIDENT
COLLISION WITH GROUND/WATER UNCONTROLLED

PHASE OF OPERATION
IN FLIGHT UNCONTROLLED DESCENT

PROBABLE CAUSE(S)
PILOT IN COMMAND - INITIATED FLIGHT IN ADVERSE WEATHER CONDITIONS
PILOT IN COMMAND - SPATIAL DISORIENTATION
FACTOR(S)
WEATHER - LOW CEILING
WEATHER - FOG
WEATHER - RAIN
WEATHER BRIEFING - BRIEFED BY FLIGHT SERVICE PERSONNEL, BY PHONE
WEATHER FORECAST - FORECAST SUBSTANTIALLY CORRECT

SKY CONDITION
OBSCURATION
VISIBILITY AT ACCIDENT SITE
2 MILES OR LESS
OBSTRUCTIONS TO VISION AT ACCIDENT SITE
FOG
WIND DIRECTION-DEGREES
130
TYPE OF WEATHER CONDITIONS
IFR
REMARKS- PILOT CERT. REVOKED 6/16/78

CEILING AT ACCIDENT SITE
100
PRECIPITATION AT ACCIDENT SITE
RAIN
TEMPERATURE-F
42
WIND VELOCITY-KNOTS
10
TYPE OF FLIGHT PLAN
NONE

FILE	DATE	LOCATION	AIRCRAFT DATA	INJURIES F S M/N	FLIGHT PURPOSE	PILOT DATA
3-3905	12/18/78	VIRGINIA,NE	PIPER PA-32	CR- 1 0 0	NONCOMMERCIAL	PRIVATE, AGE 31, 134
	TIME - 063R		N4757S	PX- 2 0 0	PLEASURE/PERSONAL TRANSP	TOTAL HOURS, 55 IN TYPE,
			DAMAGE-DESTROYED			NOT INSTRUMENT RATED.

DEPARTURE POINT
BEATRICE,NE
INTENDED DESTINATION
TECUMSEH,NE

TYPE OF ACCIDENT
COLLISION WITH GROUND/WATER UNCONTROLLED

PHASE OF OPERATION
IN FLIGHT UNCONTROLLED DESCENT

PROBABLE CAUSE(S)
PILOT IN COMMAND - CONTINUED VFR FLIGHT INTO ADVERSE WEATHER CONDITIONS
PILOT IN COMMAND - SPATIAL DISORIENTATION
FACTOR(S)
WEATHER - OTHER
WEATHER BRIEFING - NO RECORD OF BRIEFING RECEIVED

SKY CONDITION
OVERCAST
VISIBILITY AT ACCIDENT SITE
UNKNOWN/NOT REPORTED
OBSTRUCTIONS TO VISION AT ACCIDENT SITE
UNKNOWN/NOT REPORTED
TYPE OF FLIGHT PLAN
NONE

CEILING AT ACCIDENT SITE
UNKNOWN/NOT REPORTED
PRECIPITATION AT ACCIDENT SITE
NONE
TYPE OF WEATHER CONDITIONS
UNKNOWN/NOT REPORTED

REMARKS- RESTRICTED VIS AT NIGHT-AREA SPARSELY LIGHTED-LOW CLOUDS IN AREA.

FILE	DATE	LOCATION	AIRCRAFT DATA	INJURIES F S M/N	FLIGHT PURPOSE	PILOT DATA
3-4189	12/19/78 NR.OSHKOSH,NE TIME - 1715		CESSNA 172 N7390N DAMAGE-DESTROYED	CR- 1 0 0 PX- 0 0 0	COMMERCIAL POWER/PIPELINE	COMMERCIAL, AGE 39, 2000 TOTAL HOURS, ALL IN TYPE, NOT INSTRUMENT RATED.

DEPARTURE POINT
  OSHKOSH,NE
INTENDED DESTINATION
  ALLIANCE,NE
TYPE OF ACCIDENT
  COLLISION WITH GROUND/WATER CONTROLLED

PHASE OF OPERATION
  IN FLIGHT NORMAL CRUISE

PROBABLE CAUSE(S)
  PILOT IN COMMAND - CONTINUED VFR FLIGHT INTO ADVERSE WEATHER CONDITIONS
FACTOR(S)
  WEATHER - LOW CEILING
  WEATHER - SNOW
  WEATHER BRIEFING - OTHER
  WEATHER FORECAST - UNKNOWN/NOT REPORTED

SKY CONDITION
  UNKNOWN/NOT REPORTED
VISIBILITY AT ACCIDENT SITE
  ZERO
OBSTRUCTIONS TO VISION AT ACCIDENT SITE
  NONE
TYPE OF FLIGHT PLAN
  NONE

CEILING AT ACCIDENT SITE
  UNKNOWN/NOT REPORTED
PRECIPITATION AT ACCIDENT SITE
  SNOW
TYPE OF WEATHER CONDITIONS
  IFR

REMARKS- PILOT RCVD WX INFO BY PHONE FROM DESTINATION AIRPORT OPERATOR.

FILE	DATE	LOCATION	AIRCRAFT DATA	INJURIES F S M/N	FLIGHT PURPOSE	PILOT DATA

3-3271 4/28/78 NR.RENO,NV   CESSNA T210H   CR- 1 0 0 NONCOMMERCIAL   PRIVATE, AGE 36, 600
        TIME - 1022   N7211R   PX- 5 0 0 PLEASURE/PERSONAL TRANSP TOTAL HOURS, 150 IN TYPE,
                                            DAMAGE-DESTROYED   NOT INSTRUMENT RATED.

DEPARTURE POINT   INTENDED DESTINATION   LAST ENROUTE STOP
  BELLINGHAM,WA   PHOENIX,AZ/   RENO,NV
TYPE OF ACCIDENT   PHASE OF OPERATION
  COLLISION WITH GROUND/WATER   UNCONTROLLED   IN FLIGHT UNCONTROLLED DESCENT

PROBABLE CAUSE(S)
  PILOT IN COMMAND - ATTEMPTED OPERATION BEYOND EXPERIENCE/ABILITY LEVEL
  PILOT IN COMMAND - CONTINUED VFR FLIGHT INTO ADVERSE WEATHER CONDITIONS
  PILOT IN COMMAND - SPATIAL DISORIENTATION
FACTOR(S)
  WEATHER - THUNDERSTORM ACTIVITY
  WEATHER - ICING CONDITIONS-INCLUDES SLEET,FREEZING RAIN,ETC.
  MISCELLANEOUS ACTS,CONDITIONS - AIRFRAME ICE
  WEATHER BRIEFING - BRIEFED BY FLIGHT SERVICE PERSONNEL, IN PERSON
  WEATHER FORECAST - FORECAST SUBSTANTIALLY CORRECT
  MISSING AIRCRAFT - LATER RECOVERED

SKY CONDITION   CEILING AT ACCIDENT SITE
  UNKNOWN/NOT REPORTED   UNKNOWN/NOT REPORTED
VISIBILITY AT ACCIDENT SITE   PRECIPITATION AT ACCIDENT SITE
  UNKNOWN/NOT REPORTED   UNKNOWN/NOT REPORTED
OBSTRUCTIONS TO VISION AT ACCIDENT SITE   TYPE OF WEATHER CONDITIONS
  UNKNOWN/NOT REPORTED   IFR
TYPE OF FLIGHT PLAN
  NONE
REMARKS- RECOVERY DATE 7/23/78.AIRMET CHARLIE 2 STATED MOD ICING IN CLOUDS & PRECIP.MTNS OCCAS OBSCURED.

FILE	DATE	LOCATION	AIRCRAFT DATA	INJURIES F S M/N	FLIGHT PURPOSE	PILOT DATA
3-4307	8/26/78 TIME - 1705	BOLTON,NC	PIPER PA-28R N4178A DAMAGE-DESTROYED	CR- 1 0 0 PX- 1 0 0	NONCOMMERCIAL PLEASURE/PERSONAL TRANSP	PRIVATE, AGE 28, 299 TOTAL HOURS, 30 IN TYPE. INSTRUMENT RATED.

DEPARTURE POINT
POMPANO BEACH,FL
TYPE OF ACCIDENT
AIRFRAME FAILURE   IN FLIGHT

INTENDED DESTINATION
NEWPORT NEWS.,VA

LAST ENROUTE STOP
SAVANNAH,GA
PHASE OF OPERATION
IN FLIGHT NORMAL CRUISE

PROBABLE CAUSE(S)
PILOT IN COMMAND - ATTEMPTED OPERATION BEYOND EXPERIENCE/ABILITY LEVEL
PILOT IN COMMAND - CONTINUED FLIGHT INTO KNOWN AREAS OF SEVERE TURBULENCE
PILOT IN COMMAND - EXCEEDED DESIGNED STRESS LIMITS OF AIRCRAFT
FACTOR(S)
PERSONNEL - TRAFFIC CONTROL PERSONNEL OTHER
MISCELLANEOUS ACTS,CONDITIONS - SEPARATION IN FLIGHT
WEATHER - TURBULENCE, ASSOCIATED W/CLOUDS AND/OR THUNDERSTORMS
WEATHER - THUNDERSTORM ACTIVITY
WEATHER BRIEFING - BRIEFED BY FLIGHT SERVICE PERSONNEL, BY PHONE
WEATHER FORECAST - UNKNOWN/NOT REPORTED
MISSING AIRCRAFT - LATER RECOVERED

SKY CONDITION
OVERCAST
VISIBILITY AT ACCIDENT SITE
1/4 MILE OR LESS
OBSTRUCTIONS TO VISION AT ACCIDENT SITE
UNKNOWN/NOT REPORTED
WIND DIRECTION-DEGREES
90
TYPE OF FLIGHT PLAN
IFR
REMARKS- IFR,REQSTD VECTORS.

CEILING AT ACCIDENT SITE
UNKNOWN/NOT REPORTED
PRECIPITATION AT ACCIDENT SITE
THUNDERSTORM
TEMPERATURE-F
77
TYPE OF WEATHER CONDITIONS
VFR

FILE	DATE	LOCATION	AIRCRAFT DATA	INJURIES F S m/n	FLIGHT PURPOSE	PILOT DATA

3-1498 6/23/78 NR.ASHLAND,OR NAVION A CR- 1 0 0 NONCOMMERCIAL PRIVATE, AGE 54, 771
TIME - 1526 N91504 PX- 0 1 0 PLEASURE/PERSONAL TRANSP TOTAL HOURS, 100 IN TYPE,
DAMAGE-DESTROYED NOT INSTRUMENT RATED.

DEPARTURE POINT
ARLINGTON,WA INTENDED DESTINATION
VISALIA,CA
TYPE OF ACCIDENT PHASE OF OPERATION
COLLISION WITH GROUND/WATER CONTROLLED IN FLIGHT NORMAL CRUISE

PROBABLE CAUSE(S)
PILOT IN COMMAND - IMPROPER IN-FLIGHT DECISIONS OR PLANNING
MISCELLANEOUS ACTS,CONDITIONS - UNWARRANTED LOW FLYING
FACTOR(S)
TERRAIN - HIGH OBSTRUCTIONS
WEATHER - DOWNDRAFT,UPDRAFTS
WEATHER BRIEFING - NO RECORD OF BRIEFING RECEIVED

SKY CONDITION CEILING AT ACCIDENT SITE
OVERCAST 1000
VISIBILITY AT ACCIDENT SITE PRECIPITATION AT ACCIDENT SITE
5 OR OVER(UNLIMITED) RAIN SHOWERS
OBSTRUCTIONS TO VISION AT ACCIDENT SITE WIND DIRECTION-DEGREES
NONE
WIND VELOCITY-KNOTS TYPE OF WEATHER CONDITIONS
20 VFR
TYPE OF FLIGHT PLAN
NONE
FIRE AFTER IMPACT
NONE
REMARKS- ATT FLT THRU SISKIYOU PASS OVER I-5 AT 100 AGL. STRONG WINDS IN AREA.POWER LINES ACROSS HWY.

Index

Edited by Steven Messner